Praise for *Sell More with Sales Coaching*

"If salespeople had to be certified to sell, this book would be part of the licensing process! Practical, specific, solid advice."

—Dianna Booher
Author of *Creating Personal Presence* and *Communicate with Confidence*

"I love practical, how-to strategies! The real-life examples demonstrating both the good and not-so-good sales practices in this book simplifies the guidance process. This is a wonderful guide for sales coaches to get better results from their efforts."

—Tom Hopkins
Author of *How to Master the Art of Selling*

"If you would love to increase your sales, read Peri's Shawn's newest book *Sell More with Sales Coaching* and learn from a master coach of coaches. Her book is both inspiring and informative."

—Dr. John Demartini
Best-selling author of *The Breakthrough Experience*

"*Sell More with Sales Coaching* is an easy and practical way for sale managers and salespeople to increase sales by reducing 10 common sales mistakes on their way toward great sales results."

—Dr. Tony Alessandra
Hall-of-Fame Keynote Speaker;
Author of *The Platinum Rule for Sales Mastery*

"In any field of endeavor, the 'best' in the world seek out top coaches to get even better. Peri Shawn understands what makes sales people better . . . and delivers that clearly and concisely."

—Donald Cooper
MBA, CSP, HoF, Business Speaker and Coach

"The wisdom contained in *Sell More with Sales Coaching* will help your sales team 'grow their wings' so they can soar to success. Learn from Peri, one of the best sales coaches in the industry."

—Joseph Sherren
CSP, HoF;
Author, *iLead, Five Insights for Building Sustainable Organizations*

"I'm very impressed with the practicality of Peri's work! The application of her sales coaching ideas will make a huge difference to your sales. Take the ideas and run with them for the sake of your sales results."

—Warren Evans
HoF, Futurist

"While there are numerous books on selling, Peri Shawn's is by far the most useful blueprint for *coaching* your team to extraordinary sales growth. This is a must-read for sales managers."

—Jeff Mowatt
Best-selling author of *Influence with Ease*

"*Sell More with Sales Coaching* provides great insight on how to coach while making your sales team feel valued, knowledgeable and an important part of the organization and its sales growth. *Sell More with Sales Coaching* is practical, easy to use, and relevant for today's sales environment. Peri Shawn uses great analogies not only to make it an enjoyable read, but also to drive the sales coaching point home."

—**Suzanne F. Stevens**
Chief Edge Optimizer, Ignite Excellence Inc. Group

"This book delivers a proven blueprint to foster a quiet confidence to shift activity to productivity. Your team will close more sales, more often for more money".

—**Tim Breithaupt**
Author of Canadian best seller, *Take This Job and Love It:*
The Joys of Professional Selling

"Peri has taken her vast experience and made it immediately accessible. This is a very practical resource for sales managers."

—**Adrian Davis**
Keynote Speaker, Consultant;
Author of *Human-to-Human Selling*

"Peri shares her extensive and highly effective sales coaching experience in a practical guidebook filled with real world examples and how-to steps. Apply the powerful approaches in this book to truly sell more with sales coaching!"

—**Jim Clemmer**
International Leadership Author, Speaker, Coach, and Retreat Facilitator

"Attention Sales Managers – read this book! – Sales Coaching demystified and a step by step coaching plan revealed to help teams catapult sales and leave self-imposed sales barriers in the past."

—**Richard Peterson**
North America's Presentation Coach™;
Certified Sales Professional

"*Sell More with Sales Coaching* is not only written to help sales managers achieve ultimate success, it's also the 'go to' guide for salespeople who want the inside scoop on peak performance. . . . . a memorable read!"

—**Bob Gray**
CSP, HoF Memory Expert;
Guinness Record Holder

"Remember when you got your first sales management position? You wished there was one book that not only navigates the typical mistakes managers make, but point out how to leverage learning principles. With *Sell More with Sales Coaching*, your wish has come true!"

—**Tom Stoyan**
Canada's Sales Coach;
First Inductee in the Canadian Speaking Hall of Fame

SELL MORE
WITH
SALES
COACHING

SELL MORE

WITH

SALES COACHING

▼

PRACTICAL SOLUTIONS FOR YOUR
EVERYDAY SALES CHALLENGES

PERI SHAWN

WILEY

For general information about our other products and services, please contact our Customer Care
Department within the United States at (800) 762-2974, outside the United States at (317) 572-3993
or fax (317) 572-4002.

Wiley publishes in a variety of print and electronic formats and by print-on-demand. Some material included with standard print versions of this book may not be included in e-books or in print-
on-demand. If this book refers to media such as a CD or DVD that is not included in the version you
purchased, you may download this material at http://booksupport.wiley.com. For more information
about Wiley products, visit www.wiley.com.

Library of Congress Cataloging-in-Publication Data:

Shawn, Peri.
    Sell More with Sales Coaching: Practical Solutions for Your Everyday Sales Challenges / Peri
Shawn.
        pages cm.
    Includes index.
    ISBN: 978-1-118-78593-5 (cloth); ISBN: 978-1-118-78601-7 (ebk);
ISBN: 978-1-118-78598-0 (ebk)
        1. Selling. 2. Employees—Coaching of. I. Title.
HF5438.25.S4747 2013
658.85—dc23

2013027675

Printed in the United States of America.

10 9 8 7 6 5 4 3 2 1

I dedicate this book to my son and daughter.
Scott and Amira, I'm blessed to be your mother.
You both inspire me to live life to its fullest.
Thank you for sharing your lives with me.

CONTENTS

Acknowledgments   xi
Introduction   1

CHAPTER 1   Ensuring Your Sales Coaching Gets Results   3

CHAPTER 2   Sales Mistake #1: Not Being Clear
                 Who's Buying   17

CHAPTER 3   Sales Mistake #2: Forgetting Why People Buy   33

CHAPTER 4   Sales Mistake #3: Being Self-Focused   47

CHAPTER 5   Sales Mistake #4: Telling Mistruths   63

CHAPTER 6   Sales Mistake #5: Being Ill-Prepared   79

CHAPTER 7   Sales Mistake #6: Taking Too Much
                 of the Client's Time   93

CHAPTER 8   Sales Mistake #7: Sharing What's Not Relevant   107

CHAPTER 9   Sales Mistake #8: Missing Prospects'
                 Buying Cues   119

CHAPTER 10   Sales Mistake #9: Acting like a
                 Traditional Salesperson   131

CHAPTER 11   Sales Mistake #10: Treating Clients as Enemies   145

CHAPTER 12   Making Your Sales Coaching Sustainable   159

BONUS CHAPTER   Leveraging Your CRM during Sales Coaching   169

About the Author   191
Index   193

ACKNOWLEDGMENTS

I want to acknowledge my family of insightful and frank editors. Tom, Scott, and Amira. Without you this book would not exist. Your feedback was invaluable and brilliant. My bruises will go away eventually, but my gratitude lives on. Thank you.

Tom, I also want to thank you for being a wonderful example of a gifted, ethical salesperson whose perpetual focus is on helping others. Your passion for selling shines through in every atom of your being. I'm sold on you! And thank you for creating and respecting the space and time I needed to write this book.

To my dear friend and proofer, Pamela Virtue, I so enjoyed our proofing sessions that crossed the globe. Your eagle eye and friendship are deeply appreciated.

Sara Burnside Menuck, thank you for being the final editor and proofer of the book. Your gift for editing shines through. You caught important details that make the work stronger, and your professional opinion has been a great asset to the project. Thank you.

A big debt of gratitude goes to Sean Doss, the very talented graphic artist who worked tirelessly on the various graphic versions of this book. I've so enjoyed working with you. Your creative mind and vision are a gift. I highly recommend you to anyone looking to bring their ideas to light.

For the bonus chapter, thank you to everyone I interviewed. First, Rob Saul, President of Serex Sales Automation Services, thank you for having the initial conversation with me and sharing some of your resources so I could gain an overview of the CRM industry. Paul Greenberg, author of *CRM at the Speed of Light*, my gratitude to you for taking the time to express your CRM brilliance. I understand why some call you "the godfather of CRM." Gerhard Gschwandtner, founder and publisher of *Selling Power*, speaking with you was insightful. I love the pulse you have on the world of sales. Nick Stein, Senior Director, Marketing and Communications at Salesforce Work.com, thank you for demoing your Salesforce Work.com technology. I'm impressed with what you're doing to help sales managers. Courtney Wiley, Director of Global Digital Demand Generation at Oracle, thank you—your detailed understanding of how to set up a CRM was very helpful. Todd Martin, VP Sales at Pipeliner CRM, I appreciate your enthusiasm and incredible depth of knowledge about the realities of CRM and the sales manager's world. John Seeds, Marketing Director at Parature, thank you for the context you provided with your precise and thoughtful CRM ideas about how social media has changed the world for salespeople and sales managers. Rodrigo Vaca, VP Marketing at Zoho, thank you for making the time to speak with me. I appreciate your extraordinary devotion to CRM from both the customer and salesperson's perspectives and your focus on integration because of it. David Beard, CRM Principal at Sage, thank you for fearlessly diving into the sometimes murky waters of encouraging marketing and sales to work together in the CRM context. Louis Fernandes, Director, Sales and Market Development at SAS, thank you for sharing your passion for people and "the why" of business. Your CRM overview adds a nice touch to the chapter. And finally, to Mark Woollen, VP Product Marketing at Salesforce.com, thank you for fitting me into your schedule. I appreciate you sharing your rich understanding of how a strategically set up CRM can move from being just a reporting system to a sales system.

And to you, the reader, thank you for helping your team members. As much as business is measured by the numbers, business is really about people.

INTRODUCTION

S ales coaching can be the lifeblood of an organization. When done effectively, sales coaching is the catalyst that improves sales results, team morale, and employee retention.

You might appreciate knowing my sales and sales coaching biases, as they color the approach and focus of this book.

I see sales activities as a series of individual, customized conversations where the salesperson's responsibility is to help clients with their buying decisions. Salespeople start committing mistakes when they act inconsistently with this philosophy, and shift from focusing on the client experience to manipulating a sales transaction.

Use this book to more effectively coach your salespeople to help their clients with their buying decisions. As a by-product, your team members will sell more, better, sooner, and more often.

Sales coaching involves influencing your team members' *thinking*, which, in turn, improves their sales behaviors and results in greater sales. It's a cause–effect dynamic. If you try to take a shortcut, and only focus on coaching sales behaviors, you make your team members dependent on you for reinforcement. When you focus on shifting the thinking behind their sales behaviors, your sales coaching has lasting effects. Your team members are able to use the best of their thinking to solve their clients' issues and feel more confident in their growing sales abilities. And you'll feel more secure knowing how capable they are.

Coaching is both a right and a privilege for your team members, not a penance for poor performers, as some leaders mistakenly use it. Coaching is a right for every salesperson on your team, no matter what their level of sales success. And it's a privilege they earn by acting on the insights they gain from coaching.

When you effectively coach all your team members, you'll notice their sales will increase. This book is a comprehensive overview of sales coaching and its application to the most common sales mistakes. Adapt what you learn in this book to fit your team members, their clients, and your industry.

As you learn about how to apply sales coaching practices, keep in mind that effective sales coaching is much like baking a cake. The individual ingredients aren't all that enticing; the magic happens when you put them together. Imagine eating the ingredients of your favorite cake separately—two raw eggs, two cups of white flour, one teaspoon of baking powder. It doesn't sound very appetizing, does it? It's similar when it comes to sales coaching. The separate ingredients of listening, asking questions, providing information, and building trust seem quite flat to many, but when you mix them together, you have a profitable combination.

The magic of sales coaching happens when you match the coaching ingredients to the needs of each salesperson. There's a common structure to the conversation, but each sales coaching session is customized to the individual's unique needs. Imagine that each sales coaching conversation is a different kind of cake, depending on the needs in the moment. And each cake is flavored by the personality and sales skills of each team member.

You'll find I've included true stories where sales mistakes have been committed. I have changed names and identifying details to protect the salespeople (and their companies) from judgment, since most everyone is worthy and capable of rehabilitation. In some of these stories, I have included e-mails from the guilty salespeople. I couldn't have asked for better examples of what *not* to do. The sad part is: I didn't have to look hard. The stories came readily from personal sales interactions.

Today's prospects and clients are sophisticated. The ease in which product information and customer reviews and complains can be accessed is a big contributor to how people buy things. Disgruntled clients are no longer fully satisfied by filing their complaints with the perpetrating company, but instead they often vent their complaints in social media, where they live on for posterity. This makes it more necessary than ever for you to become an outstanding sales coach.

Here's to you helping your team members sell more!

CHAPTER 1

Ensuring Your Sales Coaching Gets Results

S alespeople sell more when they're coached effectively and regularly.
Results prove sales coaching increases sales, the *Harvard Business Review* has reported on it, and the Sales Executive Council documents it. Yet, you may be wondering how it works in your world.

Picture this: You have a new salesperson on your team. Joe's an average-performing sales guy, and you're about to have your first sales coaching session with him. He's just finished a sales interaction with a potential client, Susan. He's done some things well, and he's done some things that need improvement (like most salespeople).

Here's what the line graph of his sales behaviors with Susan looks like:

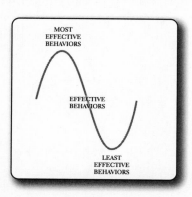

The high point on Joe's sales behavior curve represents the most effective behaviors he engaged in with Susan. These include:

- Asking some great discovery questions.
- Providing relevant information at the ideal time in the conversation.
- Remembering to set the agenda for the next time they meet.

The low point represents the least effective behaviors Joe demonstrated with Susan. These involve:

- Forgetting to ask Susan which product solutions her company had tried unsuccessfully.
- Agreeing the product he suggested was expensive without illustrating its valuable ROI.
- Not sharing the success story of a client with a similar issue to Susan's company.

Despite Joe's efforts, Susan decided not to buy during their sales interaction.

The magic happens after you coach Joe and he sells to the next potential client, Maria, with an issue similar to Susan's.

During the call with that next client, Maria, Joe does not repeat the ineffective behaviors from the low point of his interaction with Susan. His techniques that, on the graph, were labeled "Effective Behaviors," become his least effective behaviors, while the most effective behaviors from his interaction with Susan now represent his average performance. Overall, the standards of Joe's sales behaviors trend upward.

And here's the most exciting benefit of sales coaching with Joe: He engages in new, even more effective sales behaviors with Maria, so his most effective sales behaviors are stronger than they were previously. Therefore, Joe sells better and sooner in his sales conversation with Maria than he did with Susan. As proof of his success, Maria decides to buy during the interaction.

Here's what the improvement in Joe's sales behavior looks like:

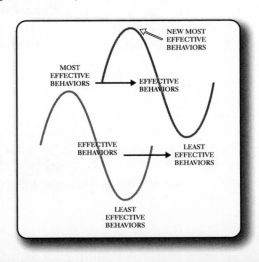

The line graph to the left shows his sales interaction with Susan, and the line graph to the right is his interaction with Maria. Imagine the sales results Joe will get when you coach him on an ongoing basis. He'll incrementally continue to sell better and sooner. *Translation: He'll sell more.*

This kind of improvement is typical for salespeople who are coached regularly. I call this the Quantum Coaching Effect. If you maintain a coaching relationship with your team members, they'll continue to reach new sales heights. You'll find they'll let go of their least effective sales behaviors and engage in more and more effective ways to help potential clients with their buying decisions.

Sales coaching can be very rewarding for sales leaders and their team members when they experience this level of improvement. It starts with your coaching focus. It's not about you being the source of all answers; it's about coaching your team to improve sales behaviors. The following story illustrates this:

With an added glint in his eye from his blade's reflection, my brother finished off his third victim. And I was his accomplice. (*A melodramatic start, yes. Yet you'll find this holds an essential sales coaching lesson for you.*) You see my brother, Brad, was different. At the age of eleven, he was an entomologist (*translation: a very serious bug guy, into beetles, butterflies, moths, and spiders*).

Among the many creatures he nurtured, were monarch butterflies, which he bred in his bedroom. I remember watching in awe as dozens flew from one end of his room to the other. *Orange never looked so beautiful.*

Brad would get the monarch butterflies as caterpillars and let them mature. Every year, he and I would watch them go through their metamorphosis from caterpillar to butterfly.

When the caterpillars would reach their chrysalis stage, which is when they are in cocoons, we would patiently wait for the chrysalides to hatch. We'd watch the growing butterflies inside move around and struggle, and struggle, and struggle. Then finally each one would break free with beautiful wings and hang there before eventually flying off.

One year, Brad and I decided we wanted to help and make the metamorphosis easier on the butterflies, so when the next butterfly started to struggle to emerge from its chrysalis, Brad took out his X-Acto knife and very carefully cut open the side of the cocoon.

We waited and watched.

No struggle. *Yes!!!!!!!!!!!!*

We shared the kind of smile only co-conspirators can understand. I felt like a superhero in the world of nature. We had single-handedly saved the butterfly. I was so proud that I wasn't prepared for what happened next.

The butterfly fell out of the chrysalis with crumpled wings. It sat there and sat there, and sat there. And then, *flop*, it died.

I hate to admit this, but did it three times before we figured out that the butterflies' deaths had something to do with us. Brad went to the books, and discovered this: The butterflies' struggle gives their wings the strength to fly, and when we took away their struggle, they couldn't fly and they died. So much for being the heroes of nature.

How This Relates to Sales Coaching

Just like Brad and I enjoyed watching the butterflies mature and fly, you probably have wanted your sales team to fly; and just like we wanted to help and make it easier for the butterflies, you probably have wanted to help and make things easier for your team. Just like we thought it was better for the butterflies not to struggle, you may have thought it was better for your team members not to struggle. Just like we had good intentions when we cut open the butterflies' chrysalides with an X-Acto knife, you probably have good intentions when you give your team members all the answers because you thought you were making it easier for them. Just like we learned that taking away the struggle for the butterflies kills them, you might have discovered that telling your team members the answers doesn't necessarily improve their thinking or their sales skills.

What No Struggle Means

For the butterflies, no struggle means no strong wings, which translates into no flying. For your team, no struggle means no new neurological connections, which means the same old thinking, which translates into no flying and the same old sales results. *Not good.* Each time you tell your team members what to do, recognize you're just like Brad and me. You're killing your team members' abilities to think and sell better.

The OSF Cycle

As you've probably already discovered, it's easy not to sales coach. It's far easier to fall for the struggle and resort to providing answers. If you fall for their struggle, you create the OSF cycle. What's the OSF cycle? It's the *Oh-So-Familiar* cycle of:

- A problem arises.
- Your team comes to you for the answer.
- You give them the answer.

And next time they have a problem, they come back to you for the answer and you give them the answers. Then you are officially trapped in the OSF cycle.

Consequences of the OSF Cycle

If you get caught in the OSF cycle, your team members' thinking and sales skills don't usually improve. They become dependent on you, taking up more of your time than you would like, and they continue to get the same sales results. *Not very productive for either of you*.

Transforming the OSF Cycle

Avoiding the OSF cycle positively influences your team members' thinking and sales skills. They take up less of your time in the long run. They become more self-reliant. *They get better sales results*.

Your role as their sales coach is to help your team members make new neurological connections so their thinking is stronger and, consequently, they yield better sales results.

> Sales coaching is about helping your team make new neurological connections.

Academic research indicates that struggle is essential for improved performance. I won't bore you with citing the details, but suffice it to say, it's similar to a light switch. You don't need to know why electricity in the light switch works. You just use it *because* it works. The same holds true for the use of struggle in sales coaching. You don't need to know *why* struggle works; integrate it into your sales coaching *because* it works.

> Struggle is essential for improved sales results.

Telling Them What to Do

Does this mean you never tell your team members answers? No. I'm not talking about leaving your team members out to dry and never giving them a helpful piece of information. There are times when it is appropriate to share and provide guidance. We'll touch more on this shortly.

I'm talking about helping your team members develop their mental strength (as the butterflies developed their physical strength) so they can fly with the best of them—and surpass their sales targets.

When you hear, see, or feel someone on your team struggling, don't fall for it. No matter how rushed they may seem, no matter how long they are taking, and no matter how poorly they are doing. Instead, here's the secret: Focus on asking questions! This will instantly put you in an ideal position for sales coaching.

The goal is to ask enough questions to give your team members a chance to make more neurological connections and you a chance to determine—of all the things in your sales coaching toolbox—what will be most helpful for you to share (or not share) with your team members.

Effective Sales Coaching Looks Like This

The most effective sales coaching is about listening to your team members first. Providing information for them is a distant second. For many sales leaders, this may seem counterintuitive, but like the light switch, it works.

Just like the most effective way for your team members to sell more is to listen to prospects to determine what from their toolbox is most helpful for their prospects. The most effective way for you to sales coach is to listen to your team members while they process their sales thoughts and develop more effective approaches to use next time they're in a similar sales situation. You share additional information only when appropriate.

To help you understand what this means to the allocation of your sales coaching time, mentally divide your sales coaching time into percentages.

Your behaviors in a typical sales coaching session would be:

- Demonstrating listening: 70 percent.
- Asking questions: 20 percent.
- Providing relevant information: 10 percent.

Demonstrating you're listening (driven with your sales coaching questions) is your first and primary focus during your sales coaching conversations. You'll find your team members will often come to a sales solution that is an improvement over what they chose to do during the sales conversation. This is why providing information can sometimes be optional. They may have just needed the space to find the more effective solution rather than have you be the supplier of the answer.

While you're listening to your team members during sales coaching, you may also discover they knew exactly what to do, but they simply didn't do it. If this is true of your team members, this is another example of how your team members don't necessarily need additional information. Instead just ask them to walk you through their plan of action. We'll talk more about this later.

Think of supplying answers to your team as an optional part of your sales conversations, and instead put your focus on getting your team members to process their sales thinking, selecting more effective sales approaches, and committing to what they are going to do differently. Only if you find a gap in their knowledge, do you share relevant information.

> Put yourself in the position to be listening during 70 percent of your sales coaching conversations.

Another way to look at the allocation of your sales coaching time is from your team members' perspective. During a typical sales coaching session, your team members' behaviors should be:

- Talking and processing ideas-70 percent. (This is when you are listening.)
- Listening: 30 percent. (This is when you are asking questions and sharing information.)

When you focus on your three sales coaching behaviors (demonstrating listening, asking questions, and providing relevant information only when appropriate), you help your team members to make stronger neurological connections between their sales ideas, which improves their sales thinking. This puts them in the position to learn more from their experience and, in turn, change and improve their sales behaviors and sell more effectively.

You Probably Do This More Poorly Than You Think

Almost everyone I've worked with thinks they are better listeners than they actually are. It really doesn't matter how good a listener you *think* you are. The reality is, when it comes to measuring your listening, your opinion doesn't matter. Listening is really measured by *the person you are listening to*.

The most important element may not be the skill of listening but the *feeling* of listening. The measure of your success as a listener is based on how much the person *feels* you are listening. To help you become a better listener, let's not review techniques to improve your listening skills, but instead, let's get really practical with assessing and developing your listening, with an emphasis on how your listenees *feel* about your listening.

Where to Start

To assess your current level of listening, get feedback from your family, friends, peers, and team members. Ask them to rank your listening on a scale of 1 to 10, where 1 is a terrible listener and 10 is an outstanding listener. This will give you a baseline to measure the improvement of your listening (and give you a reality check).

Then, get live, in-the-moment critique from these same people, so you get immediate feedback. The quicker you get the feedback, the quicker you can improve your listening. As you know, it's all about the listening you demonstrate (as opposed to your listening potential).

What Your Live Feedback Could Look Like

Your live, in-the-moment listening feedback can be a simple hand gesture. Many of the leaders I work with choose a tug of the ear or a touch of the cheek. When your chosen individuals feel you're not listening as well as you could, they will raise their hand and tug their ear or touch their cheek. This response could be triggered if, for example, they notice your response indicates you didn't hear the details accurately, your words interrupt others, or your comments don't naturally fit the conversation.

This way, you get immediate feedback so you can quickly adjust your listening appropriately. And *presto*, you're on your way to listening even better (getting closer to a coveted 10 ranking).

Why Is Listening So Important?

One of the complaints I hear from many sales leaders is they wish their team members would let them know more of what is really going on, so they can be more helpful. Well, guess what? Your team members will tell you more of what is going on if they trust you. How do I know? I have surveyed hundreds of team members and my research indicates that trust is a major component of performance improvement. Yet, what is trust? And what difference can it make to your team's performance?

Here's what I've discovered: If team members trust their leader, they will share more, provide more feedback, participate more, treat clients better, and so on.

> Trust building is essential to sales coaching.

This begs the question: How do leaders develop trust? My research indicates the number-one behavior leaders can engage in to earn the trust of their team members is to listen to them. Out of more than 52 specific trust-building behaviors, listening is ranked most important. If you would like to know which specific trust behaviors will earn your team members' trust, go to www.CoachingandSalesInstitute.com to arrange to have your team take the CSI Trust Survey.

Listening to improve performance is a simple concept—and as a bonus, it easily fits your budget. Listening more effectively to your team members encourages them to share with you what is really happening and, it bears repeating, it helps them treat clients better.

What's the Lubricant?

The key to transforming behavior is your ability to ask meaningful sales coaching questions to position you to listen more effectively. Your questions are the lubricant to get the listening going between you and your team members. Without your sales coaching questions, it's virtually impossible to keep your team members talking and sharing what is going on for them.

In some ways, you can liken the importance of sales coaching questions to the importance of sales questions. Imagine if your team members didn't ask sales questions. How well would they be able to sell? They wouldn't know their clients' needs to ensure that what they would say is relevant.

Imagine if you didn't ask sales coaching questions. How would you be able to sales coach effectively? Without knowing your team members' needs, you can't ensure that what you say is relevant. *You get the picture.*

In each chapter of this book, you receive sample sales coaching questions to assist you.

Then Comes . . . What Do You Say?

After you've demonstrated your great listening (peppered with your sales coaching questions), it is time to determine if and what information your team may need. Why *if*? As I mentioned earlier, you may find by simply asking your sales coaching questions, your team members become aware of a more effective solution, and don't need any additional information.

Before we move on to supplying information for your team members, I would be remiss in my duties if we didn't talk a bit about the timing for providing information in your sales coaching conversations. I'd like to caution you: Providing what you *think* is helpful information too early in your sales coaching process is like salespeople telling clients something about a product before asking any or enough questions. As you know, this can be a recipe for a lost sale. The same holds true for sales coaching. You want to ask enough questions to get your team members thinking more deeply and to ensure that the information you are about to share is relevant to their needs.

If you've asked enough questions and you know your team members need some information, your role is to make sure it fits their current sales needs. To help them sell more effectively and profitably, provide the information in a coach-like fashion.

How You Do That

Ensure the information *is* relevant. If you find yourself doubting the relevance of the information you are about to provide, you need to ask more questions. And when you are sure your team member needs some information, ask. You do this to check that what you are about to share is of interest to them.

Delivering the information in a coach-like manner may sound like, "Joe worked out a system for that. Would you be interested in what he did?" or, "What product manual do you think we would find that information in? Shall we take a look?"

By checking their interest level for the information, you know with certainty whether it's relevant to their current needs. At the same time, you increase their engagement in discussing how the information can help them sell more effectively.

When you provide information, either give them time to process it or help them plan what they are going to do with it. This is another part of your coach-like strategy when providing information. Don't give them information without the opportunity to utilize it. As you know, just because you tell them something doesn't mean they know how to use it.

Just because you said it, doesn't mean they can use it.

Coaching your team members to practice using new information in faux sales conversations ensures they can apply the information with clients. It may mean asking them to walk you through a product demo. It may mean asking them to read aloud the new product specs step by step, explaining why this or that is important to the client. Or, it may mean you role-play the conversation they are about to have with a client.

Something for You

Each chapter of this book includes an exercise for your team members. These exercises will help prevent your team from committing sales mistakes. However, this chapter's exercise is for you. It will help you determine which sales mistakes your team has committed and where to start in the book.

Every team makes sales mistakes. The question is: Which ones are your team members committing, and how quickly can you help identify and prevent them from occurring so your team can sell more?

Start with reading over the following sales mistakes to see if any of them seem familiar to you.

1. Not being clear who's buying
2. Forgetting why people buy
3. Being self-focused
4. Telling mistruths
5. Being ill-prepared
6. Taking too much of the client's time
7. Sharing what's not relevant
8. Missing prospects' buying cues
9. Acting like a traditional salesperson
10. Treating clients as enemies

Do you recognize any of your team members' sales mistakes? If not, it doesn't mean the sales mistakes are not being committed by your team. It may mean you're like most sales leaders who don't know which mistakes are being committed by which team members.

To help identify what is happening on your team, use the Sales Forensic Evidence Audit, which focuses on the symptoms of the sales mistakes. You may recognize the symptoms more readily than the sales mistakes.

Circle all the answers that apply for you. Then go back over the ones you selected and prioritize where you will begin. Beside each statement in parentheses are the chapter numbers to best assist you.

What do you need to increase each of your team members' sales? Circle all that apply.

1. Get clients to return/take more of my team members' **calls**. (2, 4, 7)
2. Reduce the length of my team members' **sales cycles**. (2, 6)

(continued)

(*continued*)

3. Get clients moving more quickly through my team members' **sales funnels**. (2, 7)

4. Increase my team members' **close ratios**. (2, 6)

5. Reduce my team members' **unprofitable busyness**. (2, 9)

6. Increase the sales results from my team members' **sales activities**. (2, 9)

7. Increase the amount of **repeat business** my team members earn. (3, 6, 8, 11)

8. Reduce the number of **price objections** my team members get. (3)

9. Increase my team members' **quote to sales ratios**. (3)

10. Increase my team members' **conversion of prospects to clients**. (2, 4, 5, 6, 10)

11. Increase the number of **referrals** my team members earn. (3, 4, 7, 8, 10, 11)

12. Reduce the number of client **complaints on the Internet**. (5, 11)

13. Reduce the number of client **complaints the company gets**. (5)

14. Help my team members **sell more**. (3, 4, 6, 8, 9, 10)

15. Increase the effectiveness of my team members' **prospecting** efforts. (6, 10)

16. Increase the number of **sales appointments** my team members book. (7, 10)

17. Increase the number of **follow-up appointments** my team members receive. (7, 11)

18. Reduce the **length of time** it takes my team members to close. (7, 8)

19. Increase my team members' **long-term business**. (8, 10, 11)

20. Increase the results my team members get from **referrals**. (11)

As you read this book, think of your team members and which ones are committing which sales mistakes.

Enjoy your venture into sales coaching. And, as you know, the goal is not to shame guilty salespeople, but rather to prevent sales mistakes and rehabilitate perpetrators on your team. Ultimately, your team members will sell more than they did before you engaged in regular sales coaching.

Action Items from This Chapter

1. Embrace your team members' struggle.
2. Avoid the OSF cycle.
3. Work on the percentages in your sales coaching.
4. Improve your demonstration of your listening.
5. Leverage your sales coaching questions.
6. Get ongoing, live in-the-moment feedback on your listening.
7. Work on the timing of when you share information.
8. Provide information in a coach-like fashion.
9. Get your team using information.
10. Determine which sales mistakes are being committed by your team.

Sales Mistake #1

Not Being Clear Who's Buying

It's car shopping time. *Wahoo!!!*

I read the reviews. I scoured consumer reports in magazines. I scrutinized owners' comments on the Net.

You see, I have my dream car and then I have *my car*. My dream car is a Maserati. And *my car* is the one I'm going to buy. The difference between the two? The first one is on my future list and, the other, *my car*, I can justify buying.

I like *my car's* mileage. I like its service satisfaction reports from owners. I like its horsepower. (*I like fast cars. I can't help it. It runs in the family. It's genetic.*) I only have to confirm it handles well, and decide where to buy it. All that stands between me and *my car* is a test drive and a salesperson.

I have a friend, Dave, who is car-crazy and when he hears I'm going car shopping, he wants to come along for the ride, *literally*.

Dave joins me at the car dealership closest to my house. I secretly hope it's the only dealership we have to visit. All things being equal, I prefer doing my car business close to home.

A salesperson, Eric, greets Dave and me as we walk into the dealership. Eric seems like a nice guy.

Eric brings us into his office. I explain I'm interested in my car. I state I'm the buyer; Dave is joining me as a confidante and friend, but I'm the one spending the money.

Eric proceeds to look at Dave when he speaks about the car's great mileage and horsepower, and glances my way when he talks about its color and design. It doesn't feel so good. I gather Eric must have missed who the buyer is so I gently remind him. So did Dave.

We go for the test drive, and I love it. The car handles the way I had hoped, so I know my car is definitely *my car*. While I drive, Eric points out the finer details of the car: the leather interior, the heated seats, the sunroof, and so on.

Test drive. *Check*. Now, only selecting a salesperson stands between me and *my car*.

When I finish my test drive, Eric asks if Dave would like to drive the car, too. At first I think it's nice of Eric to include my car-crazy friend. When Dave is behind the wheel, Eric discusses the features of the car including the skid control, the horsepower, the torque, the great mileage of the car, the great service satisfaction reports, and on and on.

Ouch! Needless to say, I don't feel like Eric is working with me. *I trust you're seeing what Eric is missing.* I'm sold on the car but not on Eric. So I hold off buying. I tell Eric, "I have to think about it." As you know, when clients say they "have to think about it," it's code. What they really mean is your team members didn't do as good a job as they could have. Yet, I really want *my car*. Do you ever decide against buying something you're interested in because of the way the salesperson treated you?

As we say our goodbyes, I give Eric my business card. He says he'll follow up with me in a couple of days, and just as we're going out the door, Eric asks Dave for his business card. Dave thinks it's a bit strange but he reaches into his pocket and gives Eric his card.

As I walk to my current car with Dave, I reflect on how I felt Eric had dismissed me during our interaction and how I felt he was treating me as if I were stupid. *Little did I know how wrong I was.*

I was expecting Eric's call a couple of days later and wasn't looking forward to the conversation. How do you tell someone you want what they have to sell, but you don't want to buy from them? Even though his treatment of me was not stellar, I still understood he probably had goals and plans for the commission he would make. But I never received a call from Eric. Not a couple of days later. Not even a week later.

Dave did. Eric followed up with Dave two days later about Dave's plans to buy *my car*. Eric's exact words were, "Dave, I just wanted to follow up and see if I've earned the right to your business. I've spoken to my manager. He'll give you the price you were hoping for and he'll even throw in some floor mats."

Ugh! It now made sense. Somehow, Eric didn't grasp that I was the buyer.

You may say it was only one mistake on Eric's part. Yet, I did buy *my car*. I bought it from another dealership. In fact, I liked *my car* so much, my next car was the same model. And my husband liked *my car* so much his next two cars were also the same model. And some of our friends liked *my car* so much, several of them bought the same model.

Thanks to Eric, Susan (the woman who I ended up buying *my car* from and who I referred my husband and friends to) has had a nice boost to her commissions over the years.

Sales Mistake Report Form

The Offender/Perpetrator – Enter the name of the company and/or salesperson.

> *ABC Car Dealership, salesperson Eric.*

Sales Mistake Committed – Identify the mistake made.

> *Not being clear who is buying.*

Your Statement – Clearly state the facts of what happened.

> - *The salesperson missed who the decision maker was and spoke to the buyer's car-crazy friend as if he were decision maker.*
> - *The salesperson treated the decision maker poorly, as if she didn't know anything about the car even though she had done her research.*
> - *The salesperson followed up with the car-crazy friend and not the decision maker.*

Evidence – Indicate what you wanted to buy but didn't.

> *My car.*

Future Potential Business – Outline what future business you represented.

> *I would represent a total of eight of my cars (two for me, two for my husband, and four for my friends).*
> *My friends would represent even more business.*

Eric's little blunder is one form of the sales mistake of not being clear who's buying. It's the form most think of when they think of this sales mistake—not being clear who the decision maker is. More sales people commit this sales mistake than most sales managers realize.

You may be blessed with a great team who doesn't do what Eric did. Your team members may be clear about who their decision makers are, but are they clear about the other various forms of this sales mistake?

For example, how clear are they about who else is involved in the decision-making process, how clear are they about their clients' steps in the decision-making process, and how clear are they about the criteria their clients are using to make their buying decisions?

As your team's leader, are you including these various forms of this sales mistake in your sales coaching?

Here's the Problem

If your team members don't isolate who the decision maker is, they'll be speaking to the wrong people and they'll lose sales (as Eric did with me).

If your team members don't find out who else is involved in the decision-making, they'll miss speaking to the objections of the others involved, and they'll close fewer sales or delay their sales.

If your team members don't clarify clients' steps in their decision-making process . . . they'll miss opportunities to influence their decision-making, to develop goodwill and/or to close more sales.

If your team members don't clearly identify their clients' buying criteria, they'll ramble about "stuff" that is not of interest to clients and lose sales.

Are you picking up a theme here? This sales mistake affects your team's sales ratios, conversions rates, and close ratios.

What to Watch and Listen for in Your Sales Coaching

Since sales is about helping clients with their buying decisions, it's important your sales coaching includes a focus on clients' decision-making processes.

I'm often surprised by how little sales coaching time is spent on clients' buying decisions when this is the foundation of sales conversations. Many sales managers don't include clients' buying decisions in any of their sales coaching sessions. If you are one of these sales managers, seriously consider adapting a sales coaching focus on clients' decision-making processes. Do a test. Integrate it into your sales coaching for a month and watch how it affects your team members' sales stats. You will be pleasantly surprised by their results.

The Forensic Evidence

The following forensic evidence includes some of the clues left behind when this sales mistake–not being clear who's buying—is committed. Use the forensic evidence as a guideline to help you in your sales mistake detection and prevention, and rehabilitation of the offenders.

Sales Numbers and Statistics – The potential statistical evidence you would notice about the perpetrator's results.

> *Sales process ends abruptly with no explanation.*
> *Sales cycle is longer.*
> *Close ratio is lower.*
> *Above-average proportion of prospects to clients.*
> *Clients move more slowly through sales funnel.*

Observable Prospect/Client Behavior – The potential evidence of the perpetrator's prospects/clients.

> *Takes business elsewhere.*
> *Does not stay in contact with perpetrating team member.*
> *Does not respond to perpetrating team member.*

Observable Team Member Behavior – The potential evidence the perpetrator exhibits in general.

> *Uses language that includes absolutes like "always," "never," "all of them." (Someone who is prone to overgeneralizations is more likely to overgeneralize about who's buying.)*
> *Misses opportunities for more or repeat business.*
> *Can't understand why clients aren't returning his calls.*
> *Spends a lot of time trying to figure out who to talk to.*

Observable Coaching Behavior – The potential evidence the perpetrator exhibits in coaching sessions

(continued)

(continued)

> *Tends to use a broad brush, and uses absolutes.*
>
> *Has trouble coming up with specifics and speaking to specifics (e.g., perpetrator may say client was interested, but will have trouble explaining what that looks like).*
>
> *Can't answer questions about the decision maker (or goes over the answer quickly).*
>
> *Can't get into any meaningful depth about the client's decision-making process.*
>
> *Doesn't have a strategy for clarifying who else may be involved in the decision-making.*
>
> *Can't clarify clients' decision-making criteria.*
>
> *Doesn't know client's interests or concerns relative to product.*

Whether you are new to using decision-making in your sales coaching or not, you'll want to include the basics of clarifying who the decision maker is as well as the other various forms of this sales mistake. You'll want to watch for team members who are:

1. Not clarifying who the decision maker is.
2. Not determining who else is involved in the decision-making process.
3. Not isolating their clients' steps in the decision-making process.
4. Not identifying their clients' buying criteria.

By preventing the various forms of this sales mistake in your sales coaching, you increase the chances your team will better help clients with their buying decisions and therefore make more sales.

A Word of Caution

A word of caution before we get into decision-making in more detail: If your team members get into discussing clients' decision-making processes too soon in their sales conversations (i.e., before they have asked enough questions to truly understand their clients' needs), they will turn off clients.

Your team must earn the right to discuss clients' decision-making processes. This comes after clients feel your team members have demonstrated they understand their clients' needs, and after your team members have developed enough trust and credibility so clients feel comfortable sharing their reasons for buying.

Keep this in mind. Sometimes when you are sales coaching, you'll find it helpful to explore *when* your team members engaged their clients in the topic of their decision-making. As you know, it's a fine art, knowing when to shift the conversation to clients' decision-making processes.

When you are coaching your team, your questions will help them become better at asking about client decision-making at the appropriate times in their sales conversations.

1. Clarifying Who the Decision Maker Is

Some sales managers may believe that clarifying who the decision maker is feels so basic they don't need to cover this with their sales team. I'm sure Eric's sales manager thought this way, too.

You may not need to make clarifying the decision maker your primary focus, but do ensure you know how your team is doing when it comes to this mistake. Imagine how different Eric's commissions would have been if Eric's manager had included this in his sales coaching. Eric probably would have treated me better, called me back, and made all the commissions Susan enjoyed.

It can be embarrassing for team members to admit they committed this sales mistake because it feels so basic. If members of your team share they are struggling with this sales mistake in this form, do your best not to judge them. Focus on listening. Ask questions to help them with their sales conversations. Get them focusing on:

- What happened in their sales conversation that caused them to miss who the decision maker was?

- Where in their conversations they could have asked who was the decision maker?

- What could they have asked to clarify who the decision maker was?

By delving into the specifics of their sales conversations like this, you'll help your team members do better next time they are helping clients with their buying decisions.

Once you know your team is successfully clarifying who the decision maker is, then you can move on to coaching the prevention of the other forms of this sales mistake. You don't want to start on the other forms until you ensure your team is doing a good job of properly identifying decision makers.

If they haven't completed this first step in their sales conversations, it throws off the remainder of their interactions. It would be like trying to build a house on a faulty foundation. So, ensure you and your team have *nailed* (pun intended) the prevention of the first form of this sales mistake.

2. Determining Who Else is Involved in the Decision-Making Process

As you know, the people your team members are speaking with can be a myriad of individuals including:

- One of several on a team of decision makers
- The final decision maker, but there are others who influence the buying decision
- The final decision maker who wants to engage others in the decision
- An influencer of the decision-making process, but not the final decision maker
- An information gatherer for the decision maker
- And more

Because each of these individuals can affect and influence clients' decisions to buy, your team members need to be vigilant in determining who else may be involved in the decision-making process.

You'll want to start by inquiring if your team members asked if others were involved in the decision-making. I know, this sounds basic. Yet if your team members are like most, you'll find they'll benefit from you ensuring the basics are covered.

If your team members say there are no other individuals involved in the decision, ask questions about how they know, including what they asked to find out who else was involved, and what the client specifically said in response. When you ask these kinds of sales coaching questions, you and your team members will quickly identify together what they did and didn't do to help discover who else may be involved in the decision.

Often these kinds of questions will lead to more in-depth conversations about how to ask who else is involved in clients' buying decisions. Your questions can lead to enriching learning opportunities for your team.

If your team members affirm that others are involved, ask questions about how many decision makers there are and the role each individual plays. As you know, you want your team members to clearly know the difference so they can ask more effective sales questions and provide the most relevant information to facilitate the sale.

The different roles individuals can have in the decision-making process include:

- Influencers
- Equal decision makers
- Information gatherers
- Engagers

Depending on the role of the person involved in the decision-making, your team members will need to adapt what they ask, say, and provide clients. When you include how your team members can adapt what they ask, say, and provide according to the individual's role in the decision-making, you help your team leverage opportunities to develop even further goodwill with clients. Getting your team members to explore this in their sales coaching positions them to be greater advocates for their clients.

To help your team members even more, ask questions to break down the details of the roles of each individual. Your questions could include:

- How much is each individual involved?
- Which stages involve which individuals?
- What interests and concerns does each individual have?

Ensure your team members really understand each individual's interests in your product and any potential concerns they may have about buying your product.

Your team members can take several approaches when helping those involved. These range from providing additional information to offering to be present at additional meetings to coaching how to respond to the others' concerns. The best solution depends on the individual. There is no one right way to help all clients. There is only one right way for each client.

When you are sales coaching, get your team members to focus on the most effective approach for each individual. If you consistently maintain this focus, your team members will customize the way they interact with each client.

Your team members' answers to your sales coaching questions will help all of you to plot more effective and helpful paths for clients.

3. Isolating Clients' Steps in the Decision-Making Process

This form of this sales mistake can be the most involved. You'll want to ensure your team members not only understand the steps involved in clients' decision-making processes but the implications of each step.

As you know, clients' decision-making steps can be very simple, yet at other times their steps can be very convoluted and full of sales pitfalls. By getting your team members to explore clients' steps in their buying decisions, you'll help them to avoid these potential sales pitfalls and increase their chances of selling more often.

When clients don't have a clear buying process, they usually appreciate your team members sharing the decision-making processes of other clients. It can be helpful to include this in your sales coaching. If you discover your team members' clients don't have clear decision-making processes, find out what your team members asked, said, or did so they could share the steps that worked successfully for other clients.

If you find out clients have a clear process, ask what your team did to flesh out the details. With this type of inquiry, you help your team recognize clients often have not yet formulated their decision-making processes. So when your team members ask their sales questions around buying decisions, clients may be thinking on their feet.

Inquire if your team members have asked their clients direct questions of where their clients are in their decision-making (including which way they are leaning in their decision at the moment). If your team members ask these kinds of questions, it will give them feedback so they can adjust what they ask and say accordingly.

You'll then find it helpful to ask sales coaching questions to get into the details of their clients' decision-making steps, including checking on their clients' time frames for each step of the decision-making process. When you help your team members isolate specific dates and what is being decided on those dates, you increase the chances of your team making the sale.

When discussing timelines in coaching sessions, don't let your team members get away with vague answers (e.g., "they'll be making a decision *soon*.") To a farmer, "soon" could mean next season. To a corporate decision maker, "soon" could mean this quarter or next. To a person with a toothache, "soon" could mean this afternoon. As you know, time is relative and sometimes team members can become a little sloppy or creative with clients' time frames.

Finally, use coaching to ask questions about what your team did to provide the appropriate information to clients at the various steps of their decision-making. It may mean your team members review product details with their clients, or provide some additional material and links on your company site. Or, it could mean your team members join their clients in a face-to-face or virtual meeting. *You get the picture*.

When you are coaching your team members about the information they provide clients for the various stages of their decision-making, consider doing some brainstorming with them. Discuss alternative sources and types of information they could provide. It will help them better adapt to their clients' needs in their future sales conversations.

Ensure your sales coaching includes these different components, and you'll be able to prevent this version of Sales Mistake #1. You'll strengthen your team's ability to sell better and more often.

4. Identifying Clients' Buying Criteria

Often clients can add to the confusion when it comes to who's buying. For this reason, you will want to start your sales coaching sessions to prevent this mistake by asking your team members how clear their clients are about their buying criteria.

If a client doesn't have a clear set of buying criteria, you can encourage your team members to share the criteria other clients have used successfully. Sales teams we have worked with have gained great results by sharing the buying criteria other clients have used when facing similar challenges. Clients like to learn from, and buy based on, the success of others.

If your team members are struggling with helping clients clarify their buying criteria, ask questions to get your team members exploring who else was affected by the problem your product solves. This will cause your team members to discover their clients' inherent buying criteria. These will naturally come out in the conversation with these kinds of questions.

If your team members say their clients do have a clear set of buying criteria, inquire about the details. Your team members' level of listening will become very apparent as they answer these questions. The more detail your team members can share with you, the better job they did of listening.

As you ask your team members about their clients' buying criteria, you'll find it useful to look at buying criteria from two perspectives: pains and passions. Buying criteria is about what clients want to *prevent*–pains—and what they want to *get* instead—passions. Notice one is based on the negative past the client wants to avoid and the other is based on a positive future the client hopes to gain. When you coach your sales team, ask your team members questions about the two sides of each criteria their clients are using.

For example, if a team member shares during coaching that the client was concerned about money, you could ask questions about the money from the two perspectives. You may inquire about the budget the client was working with (the pain), and about the money the client wanted to make (the passion). This two-sided approach will ensure your team members are more thorough in discovering why clients want to buy and set your team members up to be more effective with what they say about the product they are selling.

You'll also want to ask your team questions about the priority of each criteria. Ideally, your team members should be able to share with you each client's buying criteria in order of priority. By asking your team members these kinds of sales coaching questions, you help them discover clients' priorities in more sales conversations, and, as a result, your team members will ensure the product information they share is more relevant.

Back to the big picture. There's an overall focus you will probably find helpful to cultivate with your team. Sales teams who advocate for their clients (in their buying decisions) create relationships of trust that cause clients to give more referrals and do more repeat business.

Another Word of Caution

When your team members help clients with their buying decisions, objections will arise. Help your team expect objections and see them as tools to help clients with their buying decisions (not obstacles to closing more sales).

In your sales coaching, you can help your team members truly understand objections are a natural part of their sales conversations (and not to avoid them). Your team members will learn how to identify, acknowledge, and address client objections well with your coaching.

The good news is that helping clients with their objections provides your team with great material for future success stories. (I can hear your team members saying, "I had a client who was facing a similar challenge, and this is how our product helped him deal with it.")

You'll know you have succeeded when your team members bring clients' objections to their sales coaching sessions and openly want to discuss how they can better use objections to help clients with their buying decisions.

What This Means to Your Sales Coaching

Your sales coaching questions put you in the position to listen to what is really going on for your team members, and to help leverage clients' decision-making in their sales conversations.

What follows are some sample sales coaching questions you could use to deal with the sales mistake of not being clear who's buying.

Sales Coaching Questions for Sales Mistake #1

"What did you ask to discover how clear their decision-making process is?"

"What steps are involved in their decision-making process?"

"What did you ask to discover the steps in their decision-making?"

"Which questions do you think were most effective?"

"What makes you think that? What response gave you that impression?"

"Which questions do you think were not as effective as they could be?"

"What makes you think that?"

"Who's involved in each step?"

"What did you do to clarify where they are in their decision-making process?"

"What did you ask to determine where they perceived you were in that process?"

"What was their response?"

"What did their answer tell you?"

"What are the time frames for each step?"

"What concerns do they have for each stage?"

"Are there any face-to-face or virtual meetings scheduled in these time frames?"

"Were there any opportunities for you to be part of those meetings?"

"What could you have done to create some opportunities for you to be part of those meetings?"

"What did you ask to find out what you could do to help them with their decision?"

"What information will they need at each step? The first step? The second step?"

"How do you know that is what they need?"

"What did you ask to find out what information they needed?"

"What other information could have been helpful to them based on their interests and concerns about our product?"

"What information might help them with engaging others in the decision to buy?"

"What other information might help influence others involved in the decision?"

"Which part of our discussion today was most helpful to you?"

"How can you integrate that into your next sales conversation when you are helping a client with their buying decision?"

"How about we check in with one another some time next week to see how adding this to your sales repertoire affects your results?"

Decision-Maker Preparation

Your team members' preparation is a great way to ensure they are clear about who's buying. Use the following exercise to prevent them from committing this sales mistake. You can receive a printable version of it at www.CoachingandSalesInstitute. com.

For each product, have your team members fill out this chart.

Product _____

Column 1	Column 2	Column 3	Column 4	Column 5
List each of the potential decision makers for this product by title or role.	What would interest the decision maker listed in Column 1 in this product?	What potential concerns may the decision maker listed in Column 1 have about this product?	What potential buying criteria may the decision maker listed in Column 1 use in their buying decision?	What questions could you ask the decision maker to address the topics of Columns 2 through 4?

Use this chart to help your team members think through and prepare for their future sales conversations, when they will better help their clients with their buying decisions.

As you help your team with the prevention of this sales mistake, keep in mind its various forms. By integrating these different forms (i.e., clarifying who the decision maker is, determining who else is involved in the decision-making process, isolating their clients' steps in the decision-making process, and identifying their clients' buying criteria) into your sales coaching, you'll help rehabilitate your team members and prevent this sales mistake being committed by your team.

Action Items from This Chapter

1. Familiarize yourself with the various forms of this sales mistake.
2. Get your team members discussing clients' decision-making at appropriate times in their conversations.
3. Determine who on your team is not clarifying who the decision maker is.
4. Assist your team with determining the types of decision makers involved.

5. Coach your team to be clear about who else is involved in the decision-making process.

6. Help your team isolate the steps in the decision-making process.

7. Ask your team members questions to discover where clients perceive they are in the process.

8. Discuss with your team members clients' expected time frames for their decisions.

9. Clarify with your team clients' buying criteria.

Prepare your team members for objections that will arise from discussing buying criteria.

CHAPTER

3

Sales Mistake #2

Forgetting Why People Buy

Welcome to my e-mail inbox. You're about to read the first few lines of a series of e-mails from Fred, a salesperson for ABC Software. The e-mails are verbatim except for the change of names. As background, Fred did not contact me in any other way.

Monday morning, week one:

> Peri,
>   Here is a suggestion from the Mary Beth Smith, our owner. I hope that you gain some knowledge from it.
>   Call me if you have any questions.
>   Thanks,

Monday morning, week two:

> Peri,
>   In addition to being an inspirational leader here at ABC Software Mary Beth, also has tons of knowledge to share.
>   Check out this amazing advice!
>   Call me if you have any questions.
>   Thanks,

Monday morning, week three:

> Peri,
>   We can all use a little help every now and then. Below is a great pointer from Mary Beth.
>   Call me if you have any questions.
>   Thanks,

For six months Fred continued to send me the same kind of e-mail every Monday morning. There were very slight variations to these e-mails but they were pretty much the same: introducing something from Mary Beth, "call me if you have any questions" and a "thanks." (Typos also varied week to week.)

In case you were wondering, I never read beyond Fred's e-mail to see what Mary Beth had to say because Fred's e-mails weren't enticing enough for me to want to read more. In fact, Fred's e-mail turned me off from reading any further.

Would e-mails like this entice you to buy? Would they create interest on your part to investigate what Fred is selling—or trust to buy from him? If you were a sales manager at ABC Software, would you want Fred on your team?

Sales Mistake Report Form

The Offender/Perpetrator – Enter the name of the company.

> *ABC Software, salesperson Fred.*

Sales Mistake Committed – Identify the mistake made.

> *Forgetting why people buy.*

Your Statement – Clearly state the facts of what happened.

> - *The salesperson sent prospect e-mails that didn't speak to why she would buy.*
> - *The salesperson's interaction with prospect did not connect with her interests or concerns.*

- *The salesperson lowered the reputation of the company by sending e-mails that provided no value.*

Evidence – Indicate what you wanted to buy but didn't.

Their software. I didn't buy it until two years later.

Future Potential Business – Outline what future business you represented.

Me, directly. If only 5 percent of those I know bought this software, it would amount to over $18,000 per year. My colleagues with their clients would represent even more.

Fred's series of bland, unprofessional e-mails is a perfect example of Sales Mistake #2: Forgetting Why People Buy.

When it comes to sales mistakes, this one is typically not one that comes to mind. Yet many salespeople commit this mistake and many sales are lost because of it. Some of your team members may be committing this mistake without you even knowing, and if they are, they are losing sales.

Even if your team members are selling, do they know why their clients are buying? For example, do your team members really understand the reasons behind their clients' purchases? Do they recognize which piece of information made the difference for their clients? And do they know what would cause their clients to buy more?

When you include why clients buy in your sales coaching, your team will close more sales.

Here's the Problem

If your team members don't know why their clients are buying, they won't be speaking to clients' needs and, consequently, will lose sales.

If your team members don't address why their clients are buying, they'll waste time chasing weak leads (as Fred did with me) and miss out on sales.

If your team members don't take the time to find out why clients are buying, they'll lose credibility and negatively affect the reputation of your company.

If your team members don't respond appropriately to clients' reasons for buying, they'll miss opportunities for creating goodwill, developing long-lasting relationships, and earning repeat and referral business.

If your team members don't develop lasting relationships, they'll be doing busy work rather than helping clients with their buying decisions.

I'm sure you're seeing it. This sales mistake affects not only your team members' sales, but also the effort they put into earning their sales. If you help prevent this sales mistake, your team will be far more efficient at getting more sales.

Another Issue

If your team members don't discover why their clients buy relative to the product they are selling, they reduce their sales to a transaction. This brings your product down to the same level as your competitors'. Translation: The one differentiator between you and your competition is reduced to price. *Not a good position for your sales team.*

Your perpetrating team members are then put in the position of responding to more price objections. They will get caught in a price objection cycle. Your role as their sales coach is to help break this cycle so your team members can have conversations about what matters to clients, not dry transactional interactions. As you read further, you'll gain insights to help your team break this cycle.

The Forensic Evidence

The following forensic evidence includes some of the clues left behind when this sales mistake, forgetting why people buy, is committed. Use the forensic evidence as a guideline to help you in your sales mistake detection, prevention, and rehabilitation.

Sales Numbers and Statistics – The potential statistical evidence you would notice about the perpetrator of this sales mistake and his or her results.

- *Little to no repeat business.*
- *Little to no referral business.*
- *Price objections are higher than normal.*
- *Quote to sales ratio is lower.*

Observable Prospect/Client Behavior – The potential evidence of the perpetrator.

- *No loyalty to perpetrating team member.*
- *No complaints.*
- *Doesn't share much with team member.*
- *Treats the purchase as a transaction rather than a personal interaction.*
- *Negotiates on price for lack of other buying criteria.*

Observable Team Member Behavior – The potential evidence the perpetrator exhibits in general.

- *Treats sales as a mechanical transaction.*
- *Focuses on selling to more clients rather than helping current clients buy more.*
- *Gets more price objections than other team members.*
- *Honestly believes people are not buying because of price.*
- *Can be less animated than other team members when talking about the product.*

Observable Coaching Behavior – The potential evidence the perpetrator exhibits in coaching sessions with you.

- *Knows the product specs and data, but doesn't seem to be able to role-play with you.*
- *Complains about the economy and the price of your product(s).*
- *Is faster at coming up with features of product(s) than benefits.*

What to Watch and Listen for in Your Sales Coaching

Because people buy for their reasons—rather than your team's or company's reason—it's important your sales coaching sessions include an exploration of why clients buy. In most corporations, very little sales coaching time is spent on discovering this, which is ironic since it is the root of every sale.

Your role to prevent this sales mistake and rehabilitate your perpetrating team members will include your watching and listening to team members who:

1. Don't identify why clients buy.
2. Don't provide clients with what they need to buy your product.
3. Do not link clients' reasons for buying to your product.

Incorporating discussion on why clients buy into your coaching will help your team members be more effective and efficient salespeople. Integrate this exploration into your sales coaching for 30 days and watch the positive effect it will have on your team members' sales results and their efforts to make each sale.

Let's Agree

If you're like most sales managers, you're probably not surprised that when salespeople listen better, they're more successful. Just like listening makes you a better coach, listening makes your team members better salespeople.

The better team members listen, the better they understand their clients' reasons for buying; and the better they are at asking great sales questions, the more their clients will share what's important to them. So just like your questions are the lubricant to your sales coaching, your team members' sales questions are the lubricant to their sales. No discussion of sales would be complete without a focus on both sales questions and listening.

Just like your listening in the coaching world is measured by your listenees, your team members' listening is measured by their clients, their listenees.

When you're coaching, you may experience that your team members demonstrate great listening with you, but your evaluation of their listening doesn't matter. It doesn't matter if *you think* they are great listeners. What matters is what they demonstrate with their clients.

You'll know the quality of the listening your team members demonstrate with clients by the depth and quality of their answers to your sales coaching questions.

In your coaching, focus on asking great questions to determine which team members really understand why their clients buy, and what they can do to be more helpful. This means not only ensuring that your team members' sales conversations are centered around the client experience, but that your coaching sessions are as well. You'll find, by adapting this client experience focus, your sales coaching will be more productive and profitable for both you and your team members.

1. Identifying Why Clients Buy

As mentioned earlier, clients buy for *their* reasons. Salespeople often forget this, and can benefit from being reminded in their sales coaching sessions.

How do you know if your team members need a reminder of this principle? Watch their behavior and language. If they start to act in ways that demonstrate it's about acting *on* clients (e.g., twisting arms to get a close), you know they will need some reminder that clients buy for their reasons. This kind of manipulative behavior might have worked in the past, but in today's marketplace, it's considered unethical by many. It's a quick way for your team members to negatively affect your company's reputation with clients.

To get your team members better focused on helping clients, coach them to understand why clients buy. You'll find another principle very helpful in preventing this mistake: People buy on emotion justified by logic. Does your team act in a way that is consistent with this principle? If your team members are like most, they probably don't.

To coach your team members to demonstrate this principle consistently, let's look at it more closely by dividing it into its two components:

1. People buy on emotion.

2. Justified by logic.

This means the primary reason clients buy is on emotion, and then they back up their emotional decision with facts and information. Do your team members reflect this when they ask their sales questions?

Let's test the idea. This would mean clients often have emotions for wanting to buy that cause them to search for some logic to justify their emotional reasons to themselves and others.

Think back to one of your team members' recent sales. What was the client's emotional reason for buying? Ahhhh . . . what might be an emotion for buying, you ask? *Great question.*

Clients buy for a myriad of emotional reasons including:

- Impressing others
- Saving money
- Job security
- Looking like the office hero
- Keeping others safe
- Making more money
- Making them look good
- Avoiding looking bad
- Preventing problems
- Saving time
- Getting a promotion

These reasons for buying, put in the language of emotion, are clients' passions and pains. Their passions are what they're moving toward in the future, and their pains are what they're moving away from in the past. The same reason for buying can be expressed as either a passion or a pain. For example, a client concerned with money could express making more money as a passion, or reducing expenditures as a pain. This kind of distinction can prove to be helpful to salespeople when identifying clients' emotional reasons for buying.

Let's bring this down to a sales conversation. Your team member, who demonstrates this principle, would ask questions to better understand the effects of the client's problem. As your team member asks questions, the client goes into more detail about the problem, and becomes more aware and connected to the emotional reasons for needing your product. Your team member is not twisting the client's arm or slam-dunking a close, but rather helping the client become more aware of the impact of the problem. And in the process, your team member becomes more fully aware of the client's emotional reason for buying.

In action, this principle helps people on both sides of the sales equation. The client becomes more conscious of the reasons to buy, and your team member is ready to help with the buying decision. Using the language of sales, they're ready to close the sale.

Up until this point, your team member hasn't provided much content, but instead asked effective sales questions and listened well to provide the client with anything they need.

2. Determining What They Need to Buy Your Product

Once team members have clearly demonstrated an understanding of the client's emotional reasons for buying, the next job is to figure out what kind of logic will help the client justify the decision to buy. Often at this point in the sales conversation, the client has made the decision to buy. Your team member just needs to find the appropriate information (the logic) to help the client complete the deal.

Many times the client is already sold. Your team member just needs to provide the logic the client needs to justify her decision to buy. Your team's logic may include:

- Product features
- Reviews of the product
- Statistics about the product
- Comparison charts about the product
- Product demo
- Primary or secondary research

Determining what specific logic clients need is a fine art. If your team members say too much, they can get in the way of the sale. If they talk about stuff that isn't important to the client, they can lose the sale.

When you are coaching your team on how to handle this part of the sales conversation, help increase their awareness of clients' cues about their interests and concerns. It becomes a matching game of which nuggets of logic apply to which passions and pains.

For example, when I started to consider buying the ABC Software from Fred, my pain was the amount of time I was taking to service my current clients; my passion was a desire to reach more people. Fred could have demonstrated that he understood my reasons for buying if he had provided me with some information about the time I would save and the number of people his software would allow me to reach. If Fred had done this, he would only have had to send me one e-mail, saving him a lot of time and effort.

By matching clients' emotional motivations to the logical information they need to justify their reasons for buying, your team members can help more clients decide to buy, which will boost your company's sales.

3. Linking Clients' Reasons for Buying to Your Product

As you know, stories have the ability to engage people's emotions and they also make ideas more repeatable. Why do I mention this now? If stories engage emotion and clients buy on emotion, it makes sense that stories are an essential part of your team's sales conversations and your coaching sessions. If stories make ideas more repeatable, it makes sense that your team would use stories to link the logic clients use to justify their buying decisions. It means clients can repeat the logic your team members share in story form.

Are you getting the picture? Stories are not just an effective sales tool. They are an *essential* sales tool. Your team's client success stories are part of the fine art of how to link clients' reasons for buying to your product. Why is this a fine art? Because it should seem effortless from the client's experience, like a professional ballerina makes the dance seem effortless to the observer.

When your team members tell their client success stories, you want to ensure they use stories that connect with their clients. The point is not to use stories for the sake of using stories, but to use true client success stories that relate to the same emotional reasons and similar logic their current clients have. It's about using what past clients have learned to help solve current clients' problems.

Over the years I've come to develop a sales story formula that works well for both clients and salespeople.

PERI Sales Story Formula

My sales story formula has four parts:

1. Problem: Your team member explains the problem their client had (e.g., the client's emotional reasons for buying, including pains and passions).

2. Expertise: Your team member describes the aspects of your product that solved the client's problem.

3. Results: Your team member shares the results the client achieved (numbers and stats are often helpful).

4. In their words: Your team member repeats the words the clients have used upon achieving the desired results.

Typically you want each one to be only one sentence. To make the formula easy to remember, its acronym spells my first name, PERI.

Please note: Clients often buy for the *results* your product provides, not the product itself. Yet many salespeople make the mistake focusing only on selling *products*. In your sales coaching, help your team members clarify the differences between beneficial results and products, and master this distinction.

Let's see the PERI sales story formula in action. You'll recognize its sales power once it all comes together. Let's take it step by step:

- If Fred had identified why I wanted to buy, he would have discovered I was frustrated with the length of time I was spending trying to help my current clients. I wanted to help even more people.

- If Fred were to review what information he could provide to help me with my buying decision, he would have realized I would be very interested in the information of how much time his product saves and how many people the software can reach.

- If Fred was looking for a true client story that linked these together, he would be looking for an example of when his client had similar issues to me, and how he had helped successfully accomplish what she wanted. He would use a client story that included:

  o Frustration because of the considerable amount of time used to help clients (pain).

  o Desire to help more people (passion).

  o Ability to reach double or more people (logic).

Using these key points to trigger Fred's memory, he comes to realize he has several clients who match these criteria and chooses to select Mr. X's story.

Would you like me to share the story with you?

Here's what Fred might have shared with me, with my comments on key points of the story in italics:

> *My client was a consultant who spent a lot of time every week writing to clients when all he really wanted to do was help more people.* [The problem, including the pain and passion.] *I showed him how he could use the XYZ part of the software in the same time each week to help both his clients and his prospects.* [Expertise.] *Within one month of using the software, he doubled the numbers of people he was helping and reduced the time he was taking to do it sixfold . . . he brought it down to 30 minutes per week.* [Results, including logic and numbers.] *He sent me an e-mail that read, "Thanks for giving me my sanity back."* [In the client's words.]

Would this story have engaged me and peaked my interest in knowing more? *You bet.*

One More Piece

There's one more piece to this. Before your team members go ahead and tell client stories, you'll want to ensure your team members have *engaged* their clients in wanting to hear their stories.

Encourage your team members to ask their clients if they would like to hear what another client did or experienced. By ensuring your team members use questions to engage clients in storytelling, you increase the likelihood clients will want to hear them. And the more clients want to hear the stories, the more engaged they will be in the content of the stories (their emotional reasons for buying, and the logic to justify their decisions). *You get the picture.*

Actually if you read back several paragraphs, you'll notice I used this kind of question before I shared Fred's story with you.

A Word of Caution

When you are coaching your team members to use their true client success stories in their sales conversations, ensure you also coach them on *when* to use them.

Too often salespeople use stories earlier in their conversations than is actually beneficial to clients. As a result, your team members can appear too eager to make the sale.

Encourage your team members first to discover each client's emotional reasons for buying and then to identify what is the best logic to provide. By making sure they do these two things first, you ensure they are not premature in sharing their stories.

What This Means to Your Sales Coaching

Your sales coaching questions can help your team members become more aware of how to prevent the mistake of forgetting why people buy. Asking your questions puts you in the position to listen to what is really going on for your team members so you can help them more fully engage their clients in buying your product.

Here are some sample sales coaching questions you could use to prevent Sales Mistake #2.

Sales Coaching Questions for Sales Mistake #2

"Tell me a little bit about the problem your client was having. What did she say about it?"

"Who does the problem affect?"

"How does it affect her?"

"What were her biggest pains?"

"What was the passion/vision she shared?"

"What element of our product can help her with her pains?"

"How can our product help her with her passion?"

"What clients have you had who have had a similar problem?"

"Tell me about that client. How did you help him?"

"What were his pains and passions?"

"Without using the client's name, what could you tell your current prospect about how you and our product helped?"

"How could you relate her emotional reason for buying to the results your previous client got?"

"Can you put it all together now in a story? Pretend I'm the client . . . tell it to me the way you would tell her."

"At what point in your conversation could you have used this story?"

"In the last week, which client could you have used this story with?"

"Can you think of another client who has had a similar set of pains and passions who you helped successfully?"

"How about you put those together in a story?" (Assuming your team member has now developed two true client stories.)

"Which of the two stories do you think is better to put into your sales repertoire for future sales conversations?"

"How about you put it to use over the next week or so and we plan to connect in seven days? What time would work for you and me to have an update on the Monday of that week?"

Why-People-Buy Preparation

Your team members' effective sales preparation can help them remember why people buy. Use this chart to help your team members better connect with their clients' reasons and logic for buying. You can receive a printable version of it at www.CoachingandSalesInstitute.com.

You'll need one page for each problem client's experience.

The Problem _____

Column 1	Column 2	Column 3	Column 4	Column 5	Column 6
List the products you offer that solve this problem (one per line).	What questions could you ask to discover if this product is the best solution for a client with this problem?	What would be a client's emotional reasons for buying this product?	What questions could you ask to discover and confirm a client's emotional reasons for buying?	What are the facts or logic that would cause a client to justify buying this product?	Which client of yours has had a similar reason for buying and used a similar logic to justify their decision to buy your product?

You can use this exercise in a sales meeting and then follow up with getting your team members to share client success stories in a more meaningful and helpful way. It's a great springboard to get your team members recognizing what a great resource their true client stories can be.

As you know, when preventing your team from committing this sales mistake, focus on these three key steps:

1. Identify why clients buy.
2. Determine what they need to buy your product.
3. Link clients' reasons for buying to your product.

This will help rehabilitate your perpetrating team members so they will sell more effectively and efficiently. Plus, if you coach them well and they really demonstrate they understand the two sales principles (clients buy for their reasons and people buy on emotion justified by logic), they will get more repeat and referral business.

Action Items from This Chapter

1. Remind your team members that clients buy for their own reasons.

2. Help your team members better understand clients' reasons for buying.

3. Leverage the negative impact of this sales mistake (more price objections) as motivation for your team.

4. Use the client experience as your measure of success in your sales coaching.

5. Get your team to understand the principle that people buy on emotion justified by logic.

6. Encourage your team members to listen for clients' pains and passions.

7. Dedicate some of your team's coaching time to matching clients' buying reasons to the best logic.

8. Have your team develop their client success stories.

9. Practice timing so team members know when to share their stories in their sales conversations.

10. Use your sales meetings as an opportunity to develop client success stories.

CHAPTER

4

Sales Mistake #3

Being Self-Focused

Imagine that you're in charge of arranging for consultants to come and speak to members of your professional association. You work hard to provide professional programming for your association members. Your responsibility is to find the best people to come in and share best practices. Because of your role, you receive calls and e-mails from various experts who want to speak to your organization.

One day, you get the following e-mail from someone you don't really know. On one occasion, you were briefly introduced to the person, but you've never really had a conversation with him. (I only changed the sender's name and the initials of the association, so you're seeing the e-mail as I saw it.)

Here's the e-mail:

> Peri, reason for my call, was talking to Larry yesterday, happended to say I was wanting to speak to an audience who get together in a nice location where I can present my mixed success/motivational/business presentation...pdf file enclosed along with my speaker one sheet for review. it is customized as well depending on the group and can be more sales/service growing your business focus as well as motivational. . . . .reason
>
> *(continued)*

(*continued*)

I have to do this and in Toronto and asap is (below). . . Larry thought I should touch base about the ABC group.

I need a place where I can invite some important prospectives clients and maybe one speaker bureau to come and hear me speak live. . .no more than 5 people in total, possibly less. . . . .I do not speak in the GTA that much and when i do,.it is usually to companies and I cant bring any guests as i am speaking about their business. I have people who want to come and hear me live in Toronto area before booking me. I am busy and traveling a lot, but need to sort this out fast hence the reason for wanting to do this as a no fee talk.

I also will sell my book and my public programs

I am looking for between 45–55 minutes to speak

I would also need a hands free mike

Larry, thought of your audience as possibly a good fit.be the judge Peri. I trust your judgement. . .I know nothing about your group at all. . . . .my best audience are sales and service people, entrepreneurs, and people growing there business.who are also open to honour as well as stuff to take home with. . . . .read my stuff, if it is a fit, and if it would it be a nice impressive place to bring some of my prospective clients where the group meets. please contact me and we can talk more, if not.thanks for considerating my request. . . . . .and no problem. . .just, please let me know who may fit the bill instead, I will do this one for no fee as long as my requirements are met, I feel that is very fair and a win win.

Regards William

If you received this e-mail, would you buy what William is selling? Would you feel confident about having him speak to your group? Even if it was free?

Let me give you some additional context. William is a sales consultant. Did he demonstrate he had your membership's best interests in mind? Or did he demonstrate his own best interests? To help you identify the specifics of how William didn't demonstrate his sales expertise, review the number of times he used the word "I" versus the word "you."

I went back to the e-mail and counted the number of times he used the words "I," "me," or "my." Then I counted the number of times he used the word "you" or "your." I count 19 I's, 10 my's, 5 me's, and only 4 your's with no you's. That's more than an 8:1 self-focused ratio. It's not surprising his e-mail felt self-serving.

Sales Mistake Report Form

The Offender/Perpetrator – Enter the name of the company.

> *Sales consultant William.*

Sales Mistake Committed – Identify the mistake made.

> *Being self-focused.*

Your Statement – Clearly state the facts of what happened.

> - *The salesperson focused on his needs rather than his client's.*
> - *The salesperson made no effort to demonstrate he had the client's best interests in mind.*

Evidence – Indicate what you wanted to buy but didn't.

> *His speaking services.*

Future Potential Business – Outline what future business you represented.

> - *Me, directly—I would represent one event.*
> - *My association colleagues would represent enough business to keep him very busy.*

More salespeople commit this mistake than you would probably expect. William is living proof. His e-mail is a great example of the sales mistake of being self-focused.

You would not expect someone in the sales-consulting industry to commit this mistake, just as you wouldn't expect your team members to. Be aware of the expectations you have when you are sales coaching. These kinds of expectations can lead to assumptions that can cause sales leaders to take shortcuts in their sales coaching.

As you can well imagine, this sales mistake is a prospect repellent. It causes prospects to move on quickly. They may not be able to say specifically why. They just know something doesn't feel quite right.

Your team members may not be as blatant as William was in the ways they commit this mistake. Here are some questions to help you determine the degree to which your team members are committing this mistake: Do you know how clients perceive your team members in their sales conversations? Do your team members clearly demonstrate they have clients' best interests in mind? Are they more self-focused than client-focused in their sales conversations? And dare I ask: What do they demonstrate in their e-mails and voice messages? Are they more self-focused or client-focused?

If you are like most sales managers, you probably can't answer these questions because you haven't heard or seen many, if any, of your team's sales conversations, e-mails, or voice messages. Not to worry. This chapter will help you coach your team more effectively to prevent this sales mistake from being committed by your team.

If, in your sales coaching, you include the different ways your team members communicate with clients, you can better identify the perpetrators of this mistake. This will help you prevent this from happening on your sales team.

Here's the Problem

If your team members are self-focused in their sales conversations . . . they'll turn prospects off and won't have the opportunities to gain clients' interest in your product.

If your team members are self-focused in their sales conversations, they'll make clients feel like they don't care, and clients will take their business elsewhere.

If your team members are self-focused in their e-mails, they'll generate negative impressions before they even have conversations with prospects. Instead of starting from a neutral place, they will be starting from a negative. As you know, this is a harder position from which to sell.

If your team members don't demonstrate they have clients' best interests in mind, they'll miss opportunities to build relationships and make more sales.

This sales mistake literally stops your team members from connecting with prospects and clients. It can block your team members from getting beyond the initial steps of their sales process.

The Forensic Evidence

The following forensic evidence includes some of the clues left behind when this sales mistake is committed. Use the forensic evidence as a guideline to help you with your sales mistake detection, prevention, and rehabilitation.

Sales Numbers and Statistics – The potential statistical evidence you would notice about the perpetrator or results of the perpetrator of this sales mistake.

- *Low conversion of prospects to clients.*
- *Low sales.*
- *Few to no referrals.*
- *When accounts/territories are switched, new salespeople discover a significant number of interested buyers.*

Observable Prospect/Client Behavior – The potential evidence of the perpetrator's prospects/clients.

- *Takes business elsewhere.*
- *Does not respond to team member.*
- *Asks for a different salesperson.*

Observable Team Member Behavior – The potential evidence the perpetrator exhibits in general.

- *Language includes the use of "I," "me," "my," and "mine," and "we," "us," and "ours" a lot more often than client-focused "you" and "your."*
- *Can be inflexible in process, or needs to have things done in a particular way (e.g., "I can see you only on Tuesdays").*
- *Not able to build rapport.*

Observable Coaching Behavior – The potential evidence the perpetrator exhibits in coaching sessions.

(continued)

(*continued*)

- *Can't share many or any details about his client's needs.*
- *Discussions about the sales conversation revolve around what he did, not what the client asked or said.*
- *Not able to articulate client's priorities or preferences.*
- *Not able to explain what he did to customize his client approach.*

What to Watch and Listen for in Your Sales Coaching

Since sales is about clients buying, it makes natural sense for your sales coaching sessions to be client-focused.

If you find yourself or your team members diverging from this focus, think of William and how he lost his opportunity to sell himself to me because of his self-focus. Use this as your catalyst to refocus sales efforts from the client perspective.

The first step in preventing sales mistakes is identifying what is occurring so you and your team can be proactive. With this in mind, be on the lookout for language, actions, and sales activities that indicate or imply your team members don't have their clients' best interests in mind.

Consider using a client lens as your filter for all your team's sales activities, actions, and tools. If anything feels like it doesn't have a client-focus, re-examine your team's approach so it better serves clients.

These are some things to watch for in your sleuthing of this sales mistake. To be self-focused, your team has to be doing a couple of things poorly. From a sales coaching perspective, you'll find this mistake, "Being Self-Focused," really breaks down into two simple components:

1. Not asking enough effective questions to discover clients' needs.
2. Not customizing to clients' needs.

Don't Fall for It

Yes, the way to prevent this sales mistake requires watching out for only two components. But don't let the simplicity of the solution take away from the importance of the skill it takes, on your team's part, to prevent this sales mistake from being committed.

As you know from the sales coach's perspective, developing good questioning skills is not always quick to acquire. It requires perseverance on both your and your perpetrating team members' parts.

Preventing this sales mistake is not a quick one-time coaching solution. Expect it to take repeated sales coaching sessions. Think of it as a series of sales coaching conversations where your team members increase their sales questioning skills over time.

Be patient with yourself and your perpetrating team members. Rehabilitation will happen if you stick to your sales coaching.

1. Asking Questions to Discover Clients' Needs

The skill of asking great sales questions is often expected of salespeople. Many sales managers don't coach this skill in their sales coaching because they expect their team members are already good at it, by virtue of the fact that they are salespeople. It's like expecting students to be good at writing exams because they're students. As mentioned earlier, be aware of your expectations and the assumptions you make because of them.

You may think your team members already ask great sales questions. And maybe they do. Yet a little coaching on the topic will let you know who is and isn't committing this sales mistake. For those who you discover are being self-focused, coach them so you prevent them from committing this sales mistake. And for your team members who are client-focused, help them ask even more effective sales questions.

I'm sure William would be shocked at himself if he reread the e-mail he sent to me—just like most salespeople are when they discover they have committed this mistake. If you discover this sales mistake is being committed by some of your team members, be kind to them. They are probably going to be hard enough on themselves. Instead, focus on the prevention of this mistake and help your team members rehabilitate themselves.

Start with the kind of questions you want your team to be asking clients. As I've mentioned before, your team's sales questions are the lubricant to get clients talking more and your team members listening better. In an ideal sales world, you want clients talking more and your team members listening well, like a sponge soaking up their information. The more your team members know about their clients' needs, the better they can help them with their buying decisions.

Please note the choice of language, "you want clients talking more." The operative word is "talking," not rambling or pontificating. Your team's sales questions can make the difference between having clients rambling on pointlessly or talking about what matters to them.

The goal is to have your team members listening to what's important to clients and developing their relationships with clients by doing this masterfully. Effective sales questions can demonstrate competency, instill trust, and build goodwill.

Set a standard with your team members that they are not to say anything about your product until they have asked their clients enough questions to know which product will be most helpful. This will instantly prevent your team members from being self-focused and put them in the position of being more client-focused.

Typically, your team will want structure around the kinds of questions to ask clients. You'll find the structure of the three Ps of questions helpful for your team members. Since clients' needs are made up of *pains*, *passions*, and *priorities*, use this natural structure when coaching your team.

As you know, clients' pains are usually their biggest driving force for purchasing, so you want to spend a fair amount of your sales coaching time on the sales questions your team members asked or could ask to find out more about clients' pains. Exploring clients' pains will also provide your team members with information about why clients need to buy sooner rather than later.

Compare this to clients' passions, which are also a driving force but don't provide the same urgency. Instead, they are often a back-up force to the pain's driving force. For example, a fellow in pain and in need of a root canal is more likely to buy sooner than a fellow with a passion for getting his teeth whitened. As a client, the fellow in pain is going to take action to buy sooner. The relief of a pain is a stronger driving force for most people than a passion. For most people, a passion doesn't always have the same urgency. (For more on pains and passions, see Chapter 2.)

Where does the final P, priority, fit in with pains and passions? You want to encourage your team members to ask priority questions to discover where each of their clients' pains and passions fit relative to one another.

By getting your team members to focus the first part of their conversations on the three Ps of asking sales questions, you naturally put them in the position of being client-focused. As I mentioned earlier, if your team members start all their conversations this way and do not say anything (ask but not tell) until after they clearly understand their client's pains, passions, and priorities, it will make it virtually impossible for them to be self-focused. With this kind of start to their sales conversations, they can only be client-focused.

By encouraging your team members to use the three Ps structure in the first part of their sales conversations, you prevent this sales mistake from happening. As mentioned earlier, it will take a series of sales coaching sessions for your perpetrating team members to master the ability to ask the three Ps of sales questions.

Consider making your first series of sales coaching sessions about improving the quality of your team member's pain questions. These pain questions will typically be the majority of your team members' questions. Effective sales coaching reflects this emphasis.

Once your team has mastered pain questions, then move on to coaching them to master passion and priority questions.

The only measure of a great sales question is the effect it has on the client and the sales conversation. So when you're coaching, include questions about how the client responded to your team members' sales questions. The real measure of a sales question's success is how effective it is for prospects or clients.

Pain Questions

When you dig into the depth of pain questions during sales coaching, you'll find it helpful to inquire about how your team members are discovering the clients' deeper reasons for buying. You'll also find it helps team members if you explore if they are accepting superficial explanations from clients. You'll know by the level of detail your team members are able to share. If they say something to the effect of "they need our product" and can't describe why, then you'll want to use your sales coaching to help them ask better quality pain questions.

Ideally, you want your team members asking about clients' pains in enough detail so they can be helpful, and in enough detail so clients get connected to their reasons for wanting to buy. As clients talk about their pain, they will become more aware of the troubles the situation caused and will be more inclined to buy.

To help your team members with asking more effective pain questions, you'll find it helpful to ask them about the sales questions they asked:

- The effects of the pain (this can include costs, time, quality, and results).
- Who is affected by the pain? (This could include the client as well as others.)
- The impact if the pain continues. (This will give your team members more specifics of the pain and its impact on their future, including the client's reasons for buying now.)
- The benefits if pain were to end (this will give your team members their client's goals).
- What the client did to deal with the pain (this will give your team members a sense of what not to do with the client).

By breaking the pain questions down into its smaller components, you help your team members to focus better on their clients' needs.

One More Type of Question to Consider

There's one more category of questions you'll want your team members to be asking. They will demonstrate their competence to clients.

These are the questions that are specific to your industry and your client base. They cause clients first to think and then to realize they are dealing with someone who is credible. Your team members will develop stronger relationships with these types of questions.

This reminds me of a fellow working at the fruit market when I was looking at their pile of mangos. He asked me, "Are you looking for today mangoes, tomorrow mangoes, or Sunday mangoes?" At first, I wasn't sure what he meant until he proceeded to pick up individual mangos saying, "This mango is good for today. This mango is good for tomorrow. When do you plan to eat your mango?"

The man at the fruit market clearly demonstrated he knows his mangoes. I keep on going back because he picks the best fruit based on when I plan to eat it. He knows his product.

What are the "today and tomorrow mango questions" of your industry that your team members can be asking their clients?

2. Customizing to Clients' Needs

Once your team members have asked their quality sales questions and listened to their clients' responses, they will have a rich pool of client information to pull from to customize what they say to clients. If your team members do a good job of asking sales questions, but don't use the information clients share, they will demonstrate they do not have their clients' best interests in mind and clients will perceive them as self-focused.

It would be similar to you sharing with a peer that you broke your leg over the weekend and in the next breath your peer asking you to go for a hike with him. I'm sure you might wonder where your buddy was for the last five minutes of your conversation when you told him about your broken leg.

In your sales coaching, ensure you include how your team members used the information they gained from clients.

The goal is for your team members to demonstrate they heard their clients and to use that client information in what they say. (For more details on what they can say, see Chapter 2.) When your team members customize what they say to clients, it's like a matching game. To really simplify the process, your team will share only those things about your product that match the client's specific pains, passions, and priorities. This matching also includes the titles, terminology, and phrasing clients use.

Since the matching is done on the fly, it requires your team members to listen carefully, take what clients have shared, and reflect back those parts about your product that relate to what clients said. Makes sales sound really simple, doesn't it?

Simple to say, but it is not necessarily simple to do. Otherwise your team members wouldn't need your coaching.

In Addition

There are additional ways your team members demonstrate their client-focus. In your sales coaching, consider where appropriate to ask about:

- The promises they made to clients.
- Touching base with long-term clients.
- Following up on recent purchases.
- Asking for feedback.
- Soliciting suggestions or ideas.

The measurement of your team members' success at being client-focused is based on the client's perspective. For this reason when you are asking about these additional ways, include the client's response to what your team member said and asked in your sales coaching.

Their Other Communications

Earlier I asked if your team members' e-mails and voice messages were self-focused or client-focused. Do you know what their communications look and sound like?

Going over your team members' e-mails and voicemails can be a touchy subject until you establish a high level of trust with your team. Your team members may interpret your review of their communications as micromanaging. Instead, you might want to start with a softer, less direct approach.

For example, during a sales coaching session or sales meeting, show a copy of William's e-mail to your team member(s). Ask them to read it and give you their opinion of its effectiveness for sales. You may even ask them to rate it on a scale of 1 to 10, with 1 being a really poor sales e-mail that would turn prospects away, and 10 being a really great e-mail that would cause prospects to buy.

If you use it one-on-one in a sales coaching session, ask your team member why they gave it the rating they did. Let the conversation unfold into the ways in which William demonstrated he was self-focused not client-focused.

If you use William's e-mail in a sales meeting, ask your team members to share their ratings. Make it fun. Then ask them to share their reasons for their ranking. Get into the nitty-gritty details of why William would get the score he got from the team. Get into the language William used. Get into how the client would feel reading it. Get into what they thought of William as they read the e-mail.

Whether you're using William's e-mail as a learning tool in your sales coaching or in a sales meeting, you'll find it helpful to use the e-mail not just as an example of what not to do, but also as a door-opener for the next part of the sales coaching conversation.

This next part of the conversation could be about your offering to help your team with their other communications with clients. E-mail and voicemail sales coaching rarely happens. It will probably be new to both you and your team members. For this reason, tread lightly at first. Let them be the ones who control if they decide to take you up on your offer.

You may find it helpful to start with a discussion about the communication habits they have. For example, do they have e-mail templates? Are these templates built into their Outlook? Or do they copy and paste them from Word? Would they like help developing some templates? Would the team like to share their templates? *You get the picture.*

Start at a higher, more strategic level. Demonstrate your willingness and intent to help. And once they see how helpful you have been, they just might say they need help with tweaking other e-mails.

Then do the same with your team's voicemails. I get great examples of poor sales voice messages all the time on my home line. Play one of yours for the team and use the same process as mentioned above.

The goal is to earn their trust so they'll feel comfortable sharing their communications with you in a sales coaching environment. As you know, going over the details of someone's e-mails and voice messages is not always a comfortable place for team members. By taking this softer approach, you demonstrate you have their best interests in mind.

What This Means to Your Sales Coaching

Here are some sample sales coaching questions you could use to prevent the sales mistake of being self-focused.

Sales Coaching Questions for Sales Mistake #3

"Tell me about the client. What was his driving reason for buying our product?"

"What was the problem about?" (Note: This is about the client's pain.)

"What parts of his business/life did the problem affect?"

"What were the effects financially?"

"What were the effects time-wise?"

"What were the effects to the quality and final results?"

"How did the problem affect him personally/professionally?"

"Who else did the problem affect?"

"What questions did you ask to discover the details about the problem he had been facing?"

"If the problem continues, what will be the impact on him and his _____?"

"If the problem goes away, what will the benefits be to him?"

"If the problem goes away, what will be the benefits to the others he mentioned?"

"What has he tried before to deal with the problem?"

"Of the things he tried, which ones worked well?"

"Of the things he tried, which ones didn't work so well?"

"What questions did you ask to discover these details about the problem?"

"Did you get a chance to ask about what he is working toward—his vision?" (Note: The sales questions are now moving to the client's passion.)

"Tell me about his vision. How clear is it for him?"

"Does he have time frames attached to it?"

"What are his time frames?"

"Are they doable based on what you have seen your past clients accomplish with our product?"

"What else did he tell you about what he is working toward?"

"Is that doable with what you know about our product?"

"With his ideal time frames, is there anything that isn't doable based on what you know?"

"What questions did you ask to find out about what he is working towards?"

"Now . . . based on the other things on his plate, where does getting this problem fixed fit on his list of priorities?" (Note: After the pain and passion sales coaching questions, the sales coaching conversation then moves on to where things fit on the client's list of priorities.)

"What did you ask to discover his priorities?"

"Of all the questions you asked, which types of questions do you think were best for him?"

"Of all questions you asked, which ones do you think could do with some polishing?"

"How come?"

"Would you like to do some brainstorming on alternative questions you could have asked?"

"Of all of our brainstormed questions, which ones speak to you most?"

"Which ones could you use in the next week or so?"

"How about this? You test them out this week and we'll touch base and see how it went. Work for you?"

Client-Focused Preparation

You can help your team members be more client-focused by getting them to spend some time on their sales preparation. Specifically, get them working on the sales questions they can ask.

Use the following exercise to prevent your team members from committing this sales mistake by developing their sales questions. You can receive a printable version of it at www.CoachingandSalesInstitute.com.

For each client problem, get your team members to fill out this chart.

Problem Client Had _____

Column 1	Column 2	Column 3	Column 4	Column 5
What questions could you ask to discover the effects of this problem? (time, cost, quality, results)	What questions could you ask to discover who was/is affected by the problem? (Include who and how they were affected.)	What questions could you ask to discover the impact if the problem continued? (Include specific future concerns.)	What questions could you ask to discover the benefits if the problem went away?	What questions could you ask to discover what the client had done to deal with the problem in the past? (Include what worked and didn't work.)

This chart will help your team members ask better questions so they won't commit this sales mistake. If they use the questions they write out in their sales conversations, they will naturally be positioned to focus on clients' needs.

As you help your team members prevent being self-focused, leverage a two-pronged approach, coaching the questions your team members ask, and the customization they do in the conversation that follows. Be patient with yourself and your team members as they develop their questioning skills. It will take time. Your team members will not be rehabilitated in one sales coaching session. It will take a series of sales coaching conversations.

Action Items from This Chapter

1. Embrace the simplicity of the solution to prevent this sales mistake.
2. Be patient with your team members when they develop their sales questioning skills.
3. Start your team's sales question journey with pain questions.
4. Then help them develop passion and priority questions.
5. Have your team develop the "today and tomorrow mango questions" in your industry.
6. Coach your team members to customize their conversations to clients' needs.
7. Get your team to master the matching game.
8. Leverage the additional ways your team members can demonstrate they are client-focused.
9. Use the softer, less direct approach for coaching your team's e-mails and voicemails.
10. Earn a deeper level of your team members' trust.

Sales Mistake #4

Telling Mistruths

"Hello. I'm looking for Peri Shawn."

"Speaking."

"My name is Benjamin. I'm calling to find out if you are currently using a printing company for your products."

"Is this a sales call? The reason I'm asking is I am expecting an important call about the health of a family member." (My mother has cancer and I'm waiting for a call back from her doctor.)

"No, it's not a sales call."

"Tell me why you are calling and I'll do my best to help as quickly as I can."

"I'm calling to find out which company you currently use for printing your products. Do you have any products?"

"Yes, I do. In fact, I have quite a few. But this sounds like a sales call."

"No, it's not really a sales call. I'm just calling to see what you do now, how much you pay for your printing services, and maybe you'll let me quote the same projects to explore if you might do business with us."

"Benjamin, I'm going. You can call me later. Thanks." (The "thanks" is my Canadian-ness showing through.)

I end the conversation abruptly because I really want to keep the line free for my mother's doctor. Connecting with her isn't an easy task, which is why it is my priority that morning.

Back to Benjamin. He *lied* to me. He *was* making a sales call. He kept me on the line based on what I perceived to be a lie. He *was* calling to sell me something. *Not a good way to start the relationship.*

Benjamin calls back that afternoon. (I pick up the line knowing it's him, figuring whatever happens will make a great story.)

"Hello. Is Peri there?"

"Speaking."

"It's Benjamin. We spoke this morning about your printing."

"Yes, I remember." I'm saying to myself . . . be nice to the boy, Peri. *"I was pretty sure it was sales call when we talked this morning."*

"No. I was just calling to see if I could give you a quote."

"Benjamin . . . asking to make a quote would make it a sales call."

"Technically, though, it's not a sales call."

Benjamin goes on to debate that making a quote isn't a sales call. It's one of the strangest conversation starters I've ever had with a salesperson. From the client's perspective, Benjamin is starting our sales relationship based on a mistruth. *Not a strong beginning.*

I stick with the conversation because I want to see where he's going. My interest in buying from him is low, my goodwill toward him is low, and my patience is even lower. But I'm curious as to how he's going to manage the conversation from such a poor beginning. He doesn't seem like a bad guy. And he genuinely believes he isn't making a sales call.

So I play along and listen (for the sales education and entertainment value). We're 15 minutes into the conversation and it feels like it's coming to a close. I don't think there's going to be anything Benjamin can say to redeem himself or his company.

Some context would probably be helpful to you at this point. Recently, I noticed with admiration the packaging used by several of my American colleagues. I wanted to know who their supplier was. Word on the business street suggested it was a Canadian company. I had asked around if anyone knew of a great packaging/fulfillment company with no luck.

Based on this, I ask Benjamin a related question before our conversation ended. Here's the kicker: Benjamin's company *is* the supplier I was looking for! Yet because of Benjamin's poor score on my truth meter, I choose not to buy from his company.

Have you ever chosen not to buy from a company because of the salesperson's low score on your truth meter? As you know, perceived truthfulness can make or break a sale.

If your team members are like most, they are perceived as liars by some clients some of the time.

Here's my bias. I don't think Benjamin, or any other salesperson, plans their sales day with the intent of lying, exaggerating, or omitting details. Salespeople tell mistruths because of circumstances.

This is where you, the sales leader, come in. With your sales coaching, you can influence the circumstances that cause your team members to resort to telling mistruths.

Sales Mistake Report Form

The Offender/Perpetrator – Enter the name of the company.

> *ABC Packaging Company, salesperson Benjamin.*

Sales Mistake Committed – Identify the mistake made.

> *Telling mistruths.*

Your Statement – Clearly state the facts of what happened.

> - *The salesperson said he wasn't selling when he was.*
> - *The salesperson held the client on the phone based on a lie.*

Evidence – Indicate what you wanted to buy but didn't.

> *Packaging services.*

Future Potential Business – Outline what future business you represented.

> - *Me, directly—the packaging for over 100 of my sales and sales coaching products.*
> - *My professional colleagues would represent even more business.*

Benjamin committed the sales mistake of telling a mistruth. Though some may say it was a minor infraction, it tainted my trust of Benjamin and his company, despite wanting to buy their product. It was the context of the mistruth and the way he reacted to my feedback about the mistruth that made his committing of this mistake even worse.

The sales mistake is a major contributor to the poor reputation of sales. It is the sales mistake that can irritate clients. It's the mistake that often causes the clients to escalate the situation to sales managers. And it can be the mistake that gets people writing their emotionally laden complaints in social media.

As you know, social media is a place where you want people to recommend your products, not complain about them. Social media complaints are usually on the net for posterity, therefore, giving you yet another reason to prevent your team members from committing this sales mistake.

Here's a dose of reality for you. Based on circumstances, your team members will morph the truth. You can't control 100 percent of what your team members are going to say or do. But you can influence the circumstances that cause them to morph the truth.

I can hear you asking, "What circumstances would cause my team to morph the truth?" *Great question.*

Reflect on your team members and see if any of these circumstances holds true for them. Who may feel rushed? Who may feel they need to make more sales? Who may be stressed? Who may not know their products as well as they could? Who on your team doesn't like to sell?

Sound like any of your team members? And of course you saw this question coming: What are you doing to mediate the effects of these in your sales coaching sessions?

Here's the Problem

If your team members are telling mistruths, they'll turn off prospects and they'll lose sales (as Benjamin did with me).

If your team members exaggerate about your product, they'll create unrealistic client expectations, and the service department will get more complaints.

If your team members leave out important information, they'll create a cycle of client complaints that result in a poor reputation for your company in social media. And as you know, it can take a lot of effort to win back a good reputation.

Are you seeing the effect this sales mistake can have, not only on sales but on the reputation of your product and company? This sales mistake affects not only your team's sales but far more. For this reason, it is essential you prevent this mistake from happening on your team.

The Forensic Evidence

The following forensic evidence includes some of the clues left behind when Sales Mistake #4: Telling Mistruths is committed. Use the forensic evidence as a guideline to help you in your sales mistake detection, prevention, and rehabilitation.

Sales Numbers and Statistics – The potential statistical evidence you would notice about perpetrators and their results.

- *Client complaints are often high.*
- *Service department gets a lot of complaints from clients who bought from perpetrating team members.*
- *Low conversion from prospects to clients.*
- *Negative comments in social media.*

Observable Prospect/Client Behavior – The potential evidence of the perpetrator's prospects/clients.

- *Either doesn't do business or escalates the situation.*
- *Complains about being lied to.*
- *Shares negative experience in social media.*

Observable Team Member Behavior – The potential evidence the perpetrator exhibits in general.

- *Experiences added stress, and performance slips because of it.*
- *Doesn't think of consequences.*
- *Is not aware of internal processes.*
- *Creates emergencies for other departments.*
- *Focuses on immediate sales not long-term relationships with clients (some perpetrators will do anything to get business).*
- *Doesn't demonstrate he is a team player.*
- *May have trouble learning information as quickly as other team members.*

(continued)

(*continued*)

Observable Coaching Behavior – The potential evidence the perpetrator exhibits in coaching sessions.

- *Tends to have holes in his product knowledge.*
- *Doesn't know where to find answers.*
- *Doesn't have strategy in place for when he doesn't know something.*
- *Doesn't know who to go to if he needs some help.*
- *Can't explain the typical internal processes.*

What to Watch and Listen for in Your Sales Coaching

Selling is a trust-building activity. Everything else being equal, the higher the trust, the more likely someone will buy. Therefore, it would make sense to help your team members increase their trust-building activities and reduce their trust-breaking activities in your sales coaching.

Take a step further in your sales coaching by encouraging your team members to see all their actions from a client perspective, as either building or breaking down trust. Using this filter helps your team become crystal clear which behaviors to engage in and which ones to avoid.

When clients feel they can trust your team members, they will not only refer others but will become loyal repeat clients. To ensure your team is not committing this sales mistake, be aware of the circumstances that can cause your team to break down trust:

- Rushing the sale.
- Feeling an urgent need to make more sales.
- Being overly stressed.
- Not knowing product(s) or product features as well as they could.
- Not wanting to sell.

Each one of these can lead your team members to engage in telling mistruths. Include these circumstances in your sales coaching, and prevent your team members from committing this sales mistake by doing the following:

- Creating a trust-based sales culture.
- Focusing on product knowledge.
- Clearly defining sales with each team member.

In Defense of Your Perpetrating Team Members

People's behaviors are situational. A prime example would be the short response parents typically get from teenagers when asked how their day was. Yet that same quiet teenager will spend hours on the phone chatting or texting with friends about their day.

Someone observing the teenager speaking with her parents may say she's a quiet girl. Yet if someone were to watch the same teenage girl with her friends, they may say she's quite talkative. The reality is she is just a teenage girl who adapts to the circumstances.

The same is true for team members who make this sales mistake. Circumstances may cause them to tell a mistruth in one situation, but with another client, they may or may not commit the same mistake. If the circumstances are the same, they probably will commit the same mistake.

Yet from the clients' perspective (because it is their reality that matters), your team members committed the mistake and broke down trust. Clients will assume, as most people do, that this is normal for your salespeople and for your company. The responsibility for eliminating the circumstances that lead to this sales mistake lies (*pun intended*) with you. Why? Because you influence these circumstances.

It's not your team members' fault. They are often victims of circumstance.

You know the story of Dr. Jekyll and Mr. Hyde. In a nutshell, one character transforms into an evil alter ego. Under certain circumstances the same can happen to your perpetrating team members.

Let's say you have a team member named Mary Truths. She's relatively new to your team. She's been working hard at learning all there is to learn about your product, your business, and your industry. She's feeling a little overwhelmed but she spends her lunches either going over the product manuals or picking the brains of your company's top salespeople. She's well-intentioned and clients seem to like her.

During one of her appointments, a client asks her a question she can't answer and in the back of her mind she remembers you saying she has to make at least three sales a day (it's 2 p.m. and she hasn't even made one). She's feeling stressed because she doesn't even know where to find the answer.

If she's like most salespeople, she just may have some other life reasons for not performing as well as she could. For example, maybe she was kept awake last night by her two-month-old. Maybe someone in her family is not well. Or maybe she's catching a cold.

You got the idea. Mary's brain isn't functioning at its finest. In fact, brain research has shown that when we get stressed, our brain doesn't function as well. Picture this, when you're not stressed the valve that controls the flow of good thinking is open wide. When you are stressed, that valve starts to close, and slow or stop the flow of good thinking.

Because Mary is stressed, her good thinking starts to slow down and she begins to feel confused.

The client is waiting for an answer and Mary's brain is not responding well. And try as Mary may, she can't seem to access an answer that makes much sense. So her brain goes from factual mode to what I like to call "whatever-works mode." In that moment, Mary Truths transforms into Miss Truths.

As Miss Truths, she is in a sales state where you don't want your team members to be. She is in the state where she will say anything to make the sale. It's not Mary's fault. Just like Dr. Jekyll and Mr. Hyde, her change in sales state is caused by the circumstances. Mary's only human, and it's human to make stuff up when we're under pressure. It's the way we're wired.

Good news: As I mentioned earlier, you can influence the circumstances that cause your team to tell mistruths. As we walk through what you can do to prevent this sales mistake, you'll see how you can influence and affect these circumstances.

1. Creating a Trust-Based Sales Culture

Creating a trust-based sales culture starts with you. Why do I say this? Based on the way the brain works, your team members will emulate what you do. We all have brain cells called mirror neurons. These mirror neurons cause us to be influenced by the behavior of those around us. You know the old adage: You are the sum of the people you spend your time with. Science now has validated this statement.

Here's the most important part for you and your relationship with your team members: They will typically mimic your behaviors. So you'll want to demonstrate the behaviors you want them to emulate with clients.

You may be thinking, why is trust so important to a sales culture? Well, if the team members' trust of their sales leader is high, team members will tell that sales leader what is really going on, so the sales leader can be more helpful to them. The team's sales will increase as a result.

If the sales leader has developed a high level of trust with his team members, it is more likely they will emulate trust-building behaviors with clients (those wonderful mirror neurons at work). And if the team is building more trust with clients, the rate of the offenses of this sales mistake will go down and clients will share more of what is going on for them. This provides team members a better opportunity to help clients with their buying decisions. More trust increases the likelihood clients will buy. Again, because of greater trust, the team's sales will increase.

Beware

There is a downside to mirror neurons that you'll want to be careful of. If someone on your team is telling mistruths, you're going to want to make sure no one else sees it; otherwise, it can spread like wild fire.

If you have attended an event for kids, you probably have experienced the negative impact of mirror neurons in action. One child starts to misbehave and within moments the rest of the children are mirroring the same behavior. The negative behavior almost seems contagious. Sound familiar? If other members of the team get a whiff of a misleading sales technique that yields decent sales results, you can expect the misleading sales technique to spread.

When creating a trust-based sales culture, focus on the three active essentials to developing and building trust:

1. Demonstrate listening.

2. Demonstrate consistency.

3. Demonstrate that you have your team members' and clients' best interests in mind.

All three must be present for someone to have a high level of trust in another person. For example, if someone is a good listener and clearly demonstrates they have the best interests of their team in mind, yet they are not consistent in demonstrating these active essentials, trust will go down.

Let's look a little closer at the three essentials to developing trust. As we discussed in Chapter 2, demonstrating listening is about how the listenee feels, not about the degree to which the listener felt invested in the conversation. Listening is not the essential, rather *demonstrating* listening is. The quality of this listening is measured only by the listenee. Too often experts refer to listening as a skill. Yet when it comes to *demonstrating* listening, it is a *feeling*.

When you are measuring the success of your listening, pay attention to how your team members feel because you are listening to them. Do they feel you demonstrated that you listened? Do they feel you understood them and what they said? Do they feel you know *enough* to move on to solution mode?

Demonstrating consistency is about actively being reliable. For example, if you say you will do something, do it. If you say you will be somewhere, be there. If you plan to meet at a certain time, be there at that time. Consistency may seem like a little thing but it is vital to building trust.

Demonstrating you have people's best interests in mind is about doing what it takes to help others be who they want to be. For clarification, it's not about focusing on your team members liking you. If you focus on that, your behaviors may not be consistent with demonstrating you have their best interests in mind. For example, you'll probably be less likely to give timely feedback, and more likely to sugarcoat your critique (thus the team will take longer to improve). Yet if you focus on demonstrating you have their best interests in mind, you'll provide more effective feedback sooner, so they will improve more quickly. As a by-product, they'll like you.

Think of the ways you can demonstrate you have your team members' best interests in mind. Consider how you can do it with your feedback, your sales coaching and the opportunities you provide them.

And as you build your trust-based sales culture, keep in mind that your team members will emulate the same trust-based essentials with their clients. A win for you, your team, and clients.

Where do you start?

Evaluate where you are on a scale of 1 to 10 for each of the three trust-based essentials. Ask others where they would rank you on each of these and set out a plan for improvement accordingly.

You want your team to be perceived as truthful and trustworthy as possible. You want them to admit when they do commit this mistake with clients, rather than be like Benjamin who defended his position to the bitter end. Imagine how different Benjamin's sales results would have been if he had demonstrated he was listening and understanding what I was sharing with him. Help your perpetrating team members rebuild trust so the goodwill in their relationships is restored.

Bringing this back to you, I encourage you to focus on demonstrating these trust-building essentials with your team members so they will demonstrate these essentials with their clients.

These essentials also apply to how you respond to your perpetrating team members. When you're coaching your team members and you discover they have committed this mistake, demonstrate your listening. Be consistent in your questioning so you're focused on preventing the mistake, not labeling them as perpetrators. Ask them questions to trigger their memories so they can recall the information they forgot. Ask them questions to help them figure out where to find the information. Ask them questions to see if they can tell you a better way to approach the situation. These kinds of questions will help you demonstrate you have their best interests in mind.

2. Discovering Their Product Knowledge

Often when it comes to product knowledge, sales leaders focus on what their team members know. However, to prevent this sales mistake effectively, you'll want to include their ability to *use* this information in a sales conversation.

Mary Truths transformed into Miss Truths because she didn't have the product knowledge, or the ability to use it in the sales conversation with her client. Yet even if she had the product knowledge, without the ability to use it in a conversation, she would still have made the transformation into Miss Truths. When coaching your team members, check for both product knowledge and the ability to use it in a conversation.

Start by clarifying what your team members know about products. Ask them to explain to you the *what* about products. You'll also want to discover if they can use the product information in a sales conversation. You can do this by asking them to role-play with you. These two activities will help you clearly understand what is going on, and you'll know what to do in your sales coaching to prevent this sales mistake.

If your team members don't know what they need to know about products, your coaching will be around developing their knowledge. Your coaching dynamic is focused on increasing their knowledge. Ask your team members questions to refresh their memories about the products or to reconnect with its benefits to clients.

To prepare them to sell when you're not available, strategize with your team members where they can find additional information about products. Discuss who they can approach on the team who has good product knowledge.

If your team members know about a product but can't seem to have a sales conversation about it, your coaching will be focused on action-based activities and role-play. Your team members can either walk you through a conversation about the product, or you can coach your team members in a role-play.

Discover your team members' level of product knowledge and skill in communicating about products so you can determine the direction of your sales coaching. Your coaching will be more productive and effective. For example, if you discover your team member has the product knowledge but is having trouble using it in a sales conversation, you would probably ask questions to help him clarify what he would ask, do or say. You might include sales coaching questions about:

- Questions he would ask to help a client with her buying decision
- Client success stories he could use
- Relevant information he may share
- Answers he may give to a client's typical product questions
- Questions he would ask after a client decides to buy

The greater your team members' product knowledge is in both areas (information and application), the less likely they'll fall into the trap of making things up about your products. The better their strategies are for finding solutions to their lack of knowledge, the less likely they will stress and make the transmutation into Miss Truths.

By including how your team members can apply what they know in your sales coaching, their sales skills will become stronger and they'll sell more. This will decrease the pressure to rush or push sales. They will feel a sense of accomplishment from making more quality sales because of their improved skills.

Additionally, if during your sales coaching you discover team members have provided inaccurate information, encourage your team members to go back to those individuals and apologize and correct their sales mistake. Your team members can build greater trust when they take responsibility for their offenses of this sales mistake.

3. Clearly Defining Sales with Team Members

In today's marketplace, many people are taking on roles they haven't done before. Because of this, you sometimes have people in sales positions who don't like to sell. Also, you can have team members who have very different definitions of sales. For these two reasons, you want to clarify with each of your team members their definition of sales. Their definition dictates the behaviors they engage in and how they treat prospects and clients.

For example, if a team member defines sales as twisting arms to slam dunk a close (you've met this type), the way they treat clients will be very different from a team member who believes sales is about helping clients with their buying decisions. As you can imagine, the former team member will be more likely to commit this sales mistake.

It reminds me of a friend's dating experience. She had been going out with her fellow for several months and she was feeling really pressured. He was always talking about their future together, including his wish to introduce her to his family. Yet he wasn't focused on their current relationship reality; they were at the stage of getting to know one another. To my friend, it felt like he was rushing things, focused not on a relationship with her, but rather an imagined future together. She felt he was pushing her into marriage.

In a casual conversation with him one day, she innocently asked, "What's the purpose of dating?" His response: "To get married." It was then she realized why she felt so much pressure. She thought the purpose of dating was to get to know one another to see if they wanted to get married. Their different definitions of dating got them into relationship trouble.

Similar to my friend's challenge, the way your team members define sales can cause them to commit this sales mistake.

Benjamin is a prime example. It was his inability to define his behavior as sales that caused me to perceive him as being untruthful. In our conversation, he demonstrated he truly thought he wasn't selling. *Big mistake*.

Every interaction clients have with a company before they decide to buy is a sales interaction. How might that definition have changed Benjamin's approach with me? How might that definition have positively affected his relationship with me? And how might it have affected his sales results with me?

Clarify with your team members how they define sales so their behaviors are more congruent, helpful, and sales-conducive.

An Important Point

You'll find it's tough for your team members to admit they committed this mistake. Often they will feel as if they didn't intentionally lie, exaggerate, or omit details. Think of how innocent Benjamin probably felt when he told me, "Technically, it's not a sales call." Yet also think of how he might feel about the situation once he's had some coaching and he realizes he *was* making a sales call. Call it the guilt factor.

It's this guilt factor and the cultural taboos that go with lying, exaggerating, and omitting information that make it challenging for your team members to admit they are perpetrators. For them to share with you that they committed this mistake will require a great deal of trust. Trust that you'll not judge them. Trust that you won't go about telling others that they lied. Trust that you're truly there to help them.

You'll need to have a high level of trust with your perpetrating team members to help them effectively. You want to make your coaching a safe place for them to process their thoughts so they feel comfortable turning themselves in.

What This Means to Your Sales Coaching

Trust can be the leverage point for your sales coaching. Do all you can to make your coaching a safe place for them to share without judgment. Put the emphasis on their learning to do better, not on judging where they are at any given moment. Help them understand your view of their current performance as a point on a continuum of sales improvement (rather than who they are or a predictor of their future performance).

Your sales coaching questions will put you in the position to listen without judgment to what is going on for your team members. Engage your genuine curiosity and ask your questions as an exploration of what happened and what they can do better next time.

Here are some sample sales coaching questions you could use to deal with the sales mistake of telling mistruths:

Sales Coaching Questions for Sales Mistake #4
"How did things go with that client?"

"What was it that she really liked about the product?"

"What questions did she ask about the product?"

"Were there any tough questions for you?"

"What made that a tough question for you?" (Let's say your team member shares he didn't know what to say.)

"What did you tell her?" (He proceeds to tell you what he made up.)

"If you were a betting man, how certain would you be that that was accurate?" (Keep the tone of the discussion light. Let's say he says he is 50 percent sure.)

"How could we check on the accuracy of that?"

"Where might you look?" (Let's say he gets out the product manual and discovers there are some steps involved.)

"What are the typical steps to this process?"

"What steps did you include in the process with the client?"

"What steps did you not include?"

"Are there any circumstances in which we would leave out some steps?" (Notice: I softened the impact of this question by using *we* instead of *you*.)

"What would be the reasons for leaving out those steps?"

"Let's go through each one of the steps. What's the reason for each one?"

"Great. Well done. See, you *do* know your stuff!"

"How about we role-play what you could have done with your client?" (The two of you role-play the conversation and you discover he doesn't seem to be able to use some of the information about the steps in the conversation.)

"Walk me through it."

"Then what?"

"How would you say that?"

"Great."

"Now what?"

"What might you ask?"

"What would you say?"

"Did you miss any steps from your earlier list?" (Not a one . . . *Wahoo!*)

"So how will you remind yourself to do this next time you are in a similar situation?"

"Do you think you may have a need for this with other prospects in the next week?" (He says yes.)

"How about this? You use your reminder over the next week and we'll get back together to see how it went. How's next Friday morning look for you?"

"Also before we close the loop on this, do you need to do any follow-up with your client?" (You wouldn't want your team member to leave a client with misinformation, would you?)

"What are you going to do?"

"I like your approach. When are you going to get a chance to do that?"

Product Knowledge Preparation

Sales preparation is essential to prevent this sales mistake. Use the following exercise to help you and your team members understand better what they can focus on in their coaching sessions with you. This chart will help your team members clarify their product knowledge strengths and weaknesses. You can receive a printable version of it at www.CoachingandSalesInstitute.com.

Fill out this chart by putting an X in the box that appropriately ranks your knowledge of each product (or if you only sell one product each feature/option of the product you sell), according to your level of knowledge and your ability to use that knowledge in a sales conversation.

In an ideal world you want your team members' product knowledge to be excellent, but this is not a perfect world. Expect your team members to have responses in the moderate and low ranges. Your team members' self-evaluation, coupled with your experience, will direct the focus of your sales coaching sessions.

List the products you sell (or different features/ options of the product you sell)		Low	Moderate	Good	Excellent
	Your level of knowledge of the product listed to the left.				
	Your ability to use this product knowledge in a sales conversation.				

(continued)

(continued)

List the products you sell (or different features/ options of the product you sell)		Low	Moderate	Good	Excellent
	Your level of knowledge of the product listed to the left.				
	Your ability to use this product knowledge in a sales conversation.				

You can prevent your team members from committing this sales mistake by creating a trust-based sales culture, discovering their product knowledge, and clearly defining sales with each of your team members. And to keep you focused, think of the worst-case scenario for this sales mistake: clients' complaints in social media for posterity. Leverage this as your motivation for your sales coaching so you prevent this sales mistake from being committed.

Action Items from This Chapter

1. Determine which team members are experiencing circumstances that could lead them to bend the truth.
2. Be clear about the negative impact of this sales mistake.
3. Help your team engage in trust-building activities.
4. Prevent your team from making the transition to Miss Truths.
5. Create a trust-based sales culture.
6. Leverage the power of mirror neurons.
7. Clarify your team's product knowledge.
8. Role-play with your team members.
9. Get each team member to define what sales means to them.
10. Fine-tune their definition of sales.

CHAPTER

6

Sales Mistake #5

Being Ill-Prepared

My family's not normal. Sometimes on Saturday mornings, we have family outings to watch salespeople sell new products. I know, weird. You see, we have a reason for our strangeness: My husband and I are both in the sales education industry.

The day arrives. The first 3-D TV is released. My husband, true to his gender, loves anything to do with technology. He is thrilled, like a kid in a candy store, so this sales trip is serious stuff. Off we go in search of his future 3-D TV.

It is 10:15 a.m. when we enter the store. There is already a crowd around the 3-D TV. *Cool.* My husband is so giddy he can hardly contain himself. He has questions about the difference between the new 3-D TV and the latest Sony HD TV (he's a Sony loyalist).

The other people standing around the TV are taking turns with the only two available pairs of 3-D glasses. (Note to sales manager: If you are expecting a crowd to see the 3-D TV, you may want to have more 3-D glasses available.)

We wait our turn for the 3-D glasses; in the meantime, my teenage son takes off to look at the computers. (Note to sales manager: Have something near the 3-D TV to keep our attention if you aren't going to have enough 3-D glasses for us.)

A salesperson stands nearby, answering questions about the 3-D TV and monitoring who has the glasses. My husband sidles up beside the sales fellow and asks him a question. Keep in mind that we are in a store that sells the Sony my husband wants to compare to the 3-D TV. The fellow responds to my husband in an annoyed tone, "I don't know. I just walked on the floor after being away for a week. I don't know anything about the 3-D TV."

I'm not standing close by but I can hear the fellow's annoyed tone. It doesn't make me want to stick around, and my son, who is coming back from the computer section, stops in his tracks and gives me one of those teenage looks that only translates into, "What's up with this guy?"

Within moments, we are handed the 3-D glasses by the fellow, and he proceeds to tell us, "They're expensive but you get two with the TV when you buy it."

Ouch. I wonder how his sales manager would feel if he heard the fellow say the product was expensive. The fellow must have also missed that my husband, son, and I need more than two pairs of the expensive glasses. *Ouch again.*

How would you feel if the 3-D TV fellow was one of your team members talking about your product? Needless to say, we didn't buy from this fellow. Actually, we decided not to buy a 3-D TV. *After all, as the fellow said the glasses are too expensive.*

Sales Mistake Report Form

The Offender/Perpetrator – Enter the name of the company.

> ABC *technology store.*

Sales Mistake Committed – Identify the mistake made.

> *Being ill-prepared.*

Your Statement – Clearly state the facts of what happened.

> - *The salesperson didn't know his product.*
> - *The salesperson gave excuses for not knowing his product.*
> - *The salesperson demonstrated attitude.*

Evidence – Indicate what you wanted to buy but didn't.

> A 3-D TV.

Future Potential Business – Outline what future business you represented.

Directly, we would represent a total of one 3-D TV. (I can just see the big grin on my husband's face.)

Our friends would represent even more business.

The 3-D TV fellow definitely demonstrated he wasn't ready to answer questions that would sell the 3-D TV. His behavior is a perfect example of Sales Mistake #5: Being Ill-Prepared.

Somewhere, somehow, many salespeople have gotten the impression they are good enough without preparation.

Often our media perpetuates the myth that anyone can magically wake up to be a high performer, leaving out the years of practice and preparation that precede the individual's "instant" success.

Research indicates that practice and preparation are essential to improved performance. In his book *Outliers*, Malcolm Gladwell describes how practice and preparation are the creators of the great business performers in our culture.

Help your team learn that "good enough" is not good enough anymore. Coach your team members to be better prepared for their clients—better prepared to provide their opinions in a more helpful way; better prepared to answer clients' questions; better prepared to respond to client objections; better prepared to provide the information clients want and need to make their buying decisions.

Here's the Problem

If your team members aren't prepared to answer clients' questions, they'll say things that are not effective and they'll lose sales (as the 3-D TV fellow did with us).

If your team members don't prepare to respond to objections, they'll lose opportunities to use objections as a sales tool, and they'll close fewer sales more slowly.

If your team members aren't prepared to compare your product to others, they'll miss the chance to earn goodwill from clients for being proactive, and they'll lose or slow down their sales.

In short, this sales mistake affects not only how quickly your team members sell, but also *if* they sell.

When team members are masterful, it's a pleasure to watch them work. From the client perspective, the conversation seems to flow, and they get the help they want and need. When your team members are well prepared, it makes the buying process more enjoyable for clients. But when team members perpetrate Sales Mistake #5, it's painful for clients to be on the receiving end. Remember, even my teenage son, from a distance, felt the pain of the 3-D TV fellow's poor preparation.

This pain is what will prevent your perpetrating team members from receiving much business, and also reduce the odds they'll get many referrals.

The Forensic Evidence

The following forensic evidence includes some of the clues left behind when the sales mistake of being ill-prepared is committed. Use the forensic evidence as a guideline to help you in your sales mistake detection, prevention, and rehabilitation.

Sales Numbers and Statistics – The potential statistical evidence you would notice about perpetrators and their results.

- *Sales conversations of perpetrator longer than other team members.*
- *Sales cycle longer than others on the team.*
- *Low close ratio.*
- *Little to no repeat business.*

Observable Prospect/Client Behavior – The potential evidence of the perpetrator's prospects and clients.

- *Don't complain.*
- *Take business elsewhere.*

Observable Team Member Behavior – The potential evidence the perpetrator exhibits in general.

- *Prospecting efforts are not very successful.*
- *Sales conversations seem awkward.*
- *Can seem rushed.*
- *Not much depth to conversations.*
- *Sales conversations don't seem to flow.*
- *Focused more on sales activity than on improving sales skills.*

Observable Coaching Behavior – The potential evidence the perpetrator exhibits in coaching sessions.

- *May avoid being coached.*
- *No real structure to the sales process.*
- *Can't get into any depth about typical steps, actions, and strategies.*
- *Can't provide detail about preparation steps.*

What to Watch and Listen for in Your Sales Coaching

Sales broken down into its smallest components is really about asking questions, listening, and saying stuff. When you look at is this way, sales seems pretty simple. Yet your team members often stumble over what to ask or say because they are ill-prepared.

Salespeople sometimes make excuses for not being better prepared. As you know, clients don't want to hear excuses. They want help with their buying decisions.

In the case of the 3-D TV fellow, he just needed to provide enough information for my husband to justify his decision to buy the 3-D TV; instead, he gave an excuse. The 3-D TV fellow's lack of preparation caused him to say things that weren't appropriate, and that prevented him from developing a relationship with us. (Note: The fellow didn't even get the basics of the relationship going. Prime evidence is that I don't know his name because he didn't introduce himself.)

You'll notice your perpetrating team members aren't focused on building relationships with clients. They're focused on the transaction and themselves, not clients. Because of this, they do not answer client questions well and they engage in power plays with clients (instead of responding to clients' objections).

You'll find your perpetrating team members will often give their personal opinions, unconnected to clients' buying. In fact, they'll often give opinions that reduce clients' desire to buy. Remember when the 3-D TV fellow described the glasses as expensive. (*I cringed when he said it. Did you cringe when you read it?*) The fellow totally turned my husband off buying a 3-D TV.

In your efforts to prevent this mistake, watch for team members who are:

1. Giving their opinion unconnected to clients' needs.
2. Not answering questions well.
3. Not responding to client objections in a helpful way.
4. Making up excuses for not knowing information.

Get your team members focused on building relationships. This engages their clients in talking about what's important to them, creating goodwill in the process and determining what to say that will be most relevant and helpful to clients and their buying decision.

Fine Line

There's a fine line between being well-prepared and being stiff and scripted. The goal in your team's preparation is to do enough so they sell well and don't sound stiff and scripted. Part of your role is to gauge how natural and comfortable they seem. Engage your team members in a discussion about how their wording feels for them. If they say it doesn't feel comfortable, coach them to discover a different version that feels like a better fit.

Some salespeople think sales is about putting on an act. In fact, some of your sales team might have been coached to do this in a past sales life. This can contribute to your team sounding stiff and scripted.

Encourage your team members to bring their personalities to work. Help them to find their personal versions during their preparation. Get your team members feeling and sounding like themselves rather than sales robots spouting off the same lines as their colleagues. When your team members' personalities shine through, they have greater integrity. They are more animated, engaging, and helpful. These are all great behaviors for helping clients with their buying decisions and for making more sales.

Just like athletic coaching involves both strengthening and stretching, your sales coaching will involve strengthening their sales skills and removing the stiffness in their communication. *Strengthen and stretch.*

Your Coaching Will Be Different

When preventing this sales mistake, your coaching will be slightly different from your usual sales coaching. It won't be about a specific sales conversation. Instead, it will be about preparing based on past patterns and future expectations. Instead of reviewing what happened in a specific sales conversation with a client, start your sales coaching by asking your team members to reflect and share a pattern they have experienced or something they anticipate happening in the near future. For example, a pattern your team member might have experienced could be a type of objection they heard repeatedly this past week. In this case, your coaching would be about preparing your team member to respond better to that type of objection.

An example of anticipation could have to do with a particular client your team member anticipates will be asking a lot of questions about how your product compares to something being released by your competitor. Your sales coaching would be focused on helping your team member prepare to have conversations about your product compared to your competition's soon-to-be-released product.

You get the picture. Your coaching switches from being focused on a specific sales conversation to either a pattern of the past or something in the future.

Your Sales Coaching Structure

The general structure of your sales coaching of this sales mistake will look like this:

- Discover the past pattern or anticipated future.
- Coach alternative ways to handle either.

- Create ways to respond to the related client behaviors.
- Role-play in context.
- Coach to discover best wording for your team member.

When you are doing the role-play, ensure it is thorough and that your team members include:

- What they are going to ask clients.
- What they are going to say to clients.
- What information they can provide.
- When in the conversation they are going to use their new approach.

You want to be confident your team members' skill level is high enough to help clients with their buying decisions. The 3-D TV fellow shouldn't have been on the 3-D TV section of the floor with his lack of preparation—and definitely not on the day the first 3-D TV was released. Imagine how different the outcome would have been if a well-prepared salesperson was there in his place. How many 3-D TVs would have been sold that day?

1. Giving Their Opinion Appropriately

Clients today don't expect your team members to be formal. Business conversations are more casual than they once were. Yet this is not a reason for your team members to be sloppy. The casualness in business does still have some etiquette when it comes to your team sharing their opinions.

There *is* room for opinion in sales, and hearing a salesperson's opinions can be quite refreshing for clients when they relate to their interests. But there isn't room for opinions that are irrelevant for clients.

For example, let's review the opinion the 3-D TV fellow shared. His opinion that the glasses were expensive was not helpful to us. What he actually meant was, in his opinion, the glasses were too expensive for him. He didn't know or inquire if they would be too expensive for us. As you know, expensive is a relative term.

I have a friend. We affectionately refer to each other as "antiparticles." What's expensive for me is reasonable value for her, and what seems reasonable for me seems expensive for her. How does this work? What she spends on a piece of jewelry is way too expensive for me, and what I spend on professional courses is way too expensive for her. Help your team understand that the definition of expensive (or any other word) is individual, not universal.

When coaching your team to share their opinions appropriately, ensure they prepare questions to help them determine what opinion of theirs will be of interest to clients. For example, if the 3-D TV fellow was well-prepared and had asked my husband about what he was looking for in a 3-D TV, he would have discovered that my husband was interested in the techie side of the 3-D TV. In this case, the fellow might have shared his insider's techie view on the best way to set up the 3-D TV, based on his experience.

If your team members are users of your product and are able to give me some practical information to help me enjoy or use your product better, I'm all ears as a client. I'd want to hear what your team members have to say. I'd actually feel special because I'm getting information I can't get elsewhere. Sharing personal, relevant opinions is a great way to build client loyalty.

When you are coaching your team members, ensure they can share their opinions in a way that is valuable for clients.

2. Answering Questions Well

Some salespeople act as if they don't expect clients to ask questions. As obvious as it may seem to you, your team members will often need your coaching to be better prepared to answer client questions. Help your team do a better job of answering these questions by preparing them for those questions in your coaching sessions.

The first step is determining with your team members which questions they should be prepared to answer. In every industry, there are the typical questions clients ask. These will be the foundation of preparation with your team. Consider having your team develop an ongoing collection of your industry's frequently asked questions. Everyone can add their own set of answers.

Though the core of these questions will remain the same, their answers will sometimes change based on what your competition is doing, new developments in the field, and trends in the industry. You'll want to make sure your team stays up to date with the answers to these client questions.

The second step is about individual team members preparing specific responses to the questions they get the most. This preparation can be done one on one in a sales coaching session or in a sales meeting.

If you choose to go with a sales coaching session, you'll probably find it helpful to brainstorm first, then give each team member a chance to pick the answers that are best for them. If you choose to do this during a sales meeting, you'll probably want to have your team members share best practices, and then have each person select what is best for them.

Finally, the third step is about each team member practicing their responses to the questions they're asked most often. They should also tweak them until their response feels like a natural fit, while still answering the question in a helpful manner for the client.

3. Responding to Client Objections in a Helpful Way

Too often salespeople try to work *on* clients rather than working *with* them. One of the ways salespeople do this is by trying to *overcome* clients' objections. Many salespeople are under the impression that engaging in a power game with clients will get them more sales. However, you and I know that engaging in a power dynamic with clients will most likely turn clients off and lose sales. The importance of overcoming clients' objections is a myth. Clients don't want someone to overcome their objections. Clients want someone to help them with their concerns. Clients want someone working with them, not against them. This approach of working with clients (rather than engaging in a power play of overcoming objections) is part of the new sales culture you can create with your team. (For more on creating this trust-based sales culture, see Chapter 5.)

Typical client objections to prepare for might inlcude price, the product, timing, and so on. In addition to these, you and your team should discuss familiar industry- and product-specific objections.

As you coach your team members, you are preparing them to not only respond to the objection but also to:

- Isolate the objection.
- Clarify the reasons behind the objection.
- Find out more about the objection.

You do this so that what your team members say is most relevant to clients' needs.

When you're preparing your team members, you'll probably need to remind them repeatedly that they're working *with* clients and their objections, not trying to overcome client objections. Keep at it until they truly demonstrate that they get it, which is evidenced by increased performance in real client situations.

There is a category of objections I have yet to see any company prepare their team to answer. It's the category of unspoken objections the industry creates with its hidden processes or procedures. For example, many industries have hidden fees. Let's say your company, like your competitors, charges an activation fee that is standard in the industry. In your sales coaching, prepare your team for how they can leverage this objection as a sales tool, not as a client objection.

In this case, you would brainstorm with your team members what they could say to prospects about the activation fee. Then they can polish the exact phrasing that works for them. Their final wording could look something like this: "Many of my clients have said they really appreciated knowing what the billing will look like so there are no surprises. In this industry, we are regulated and there are some fees you will get on your first bill no matter who you buy from . . ."

This kind of proactive approach by your team will develop trust and position your team members as the ones to buy from. This positioning puts your team members on the same side rather than on the opposing side in a power play.

4. Knowing What Information Clients Want

Clients are more likely to buy if they receive the targeted information they want about your product. The sooner your team members can provide that information, the sooner clients will buy. So the information your team members provide, and their ability to deliver that information in a timely manner will affect their sales.

The assumption is that your team members know their products and they are able to have helpful client conversations about those products. You can determine their skill set by watching how your team members handle their sales conversations and how much they customize those conversations to clients' needs. If you want to read more about how to do this, see Chapter 3.

When it comes to the part of the conversation where your team members provide clients with information, you ideally want your team members to have the information on the tip of their tongue. In the real world, this may not always be possible. Though there are no excuses from the client perspective, from your team members' perspective, there are logical reasons for their lack of knowledge. For example, since product training is an ongoing activity, it can only be expected that, with vacations and absences, your team members will at some point miss some training. Clients don't know this, nor should they. Expect your team members to have gaps in their product knowledge and adapt your coaching accordingly. You have the ability to fill the gap between the clients' perspective and your team members' perspective. This is where your coaching becomes a critical tool.

Yet, if you put your team members in the position of interacting with clients when they are not prepared to help clients appropriately, you become an accomplice to their ill-preparedness. Please raise your left hand and repeat after me: "I solemnly swear to not let my ill-prepared team members interact with prospects or clients until they demonstrate they are properly prepared."

This oath, coupled with your sales coaching, will prevent this sales mistake from being committed by your team members.

Imagine how things would be different if the 3-D TV fellow's sales manager had made this commitment. We'd be the proud owners of a 3-D TV. Heck, they probably would have sold a few more 3-D TVs to the other people in the crowd, too. I wonder if the executives in the company who launched the 3-D TV are thinking clients just aren't interested in 3-D technology, rather than the reality that people didn't get the information they wanted from the 3-D TV fellow.

With your commitment and your sales coaching, you can ensure that your team members are able to provide clients with the information they want and need. It's not only your team members' responsibility to be prepared, but it is also yours.

Keep in mind the sales coaching structure I shared with your earlier:

1. Discover the past pattern or anticipated future.

2. Coach alternative ways to handle it.

3. Create ways to respond to patterns and anticipated objections.

4. Role-play in context.

5. Coach to discover the best wording for each team member.

In the case of the 3-D TV fellow, he and his sales manager could have anticipated prospects would be coming into the store to check out the 3-D TVs. After all, they were carrying the first released 3-D TV.

Yet you may be thinking, "How can my team members know what prospects are interested in?"

This is where you and your team members can be proactive. Your team members are a great resource. They'll know the questions prospects are asking. As mentioned earlier, use these past questions as a structure so you can help your team better prepare to provide information.

You can also leverage technology. You and your team members can use technology to listen to what prospects and clients are interested in relative to your product. You can also utilize technology to keep current on news in your industry so you and your team members know the latest information.

A few examples of how you could leverage technology would be:

- Using Twitter to listen to what clients are saying so your team members can use those comments and insights to help prospects with their answers.

- Setting up Google Alerts about you and your competitors so your team knows the latest information about both for comparison.

- Searching for reviews related to your products so your team members can have some independent information for prospects.

The information available by using technology will help your team members and their clients with their buying decisions. And the quicker and more effectively they can provide these for their prospects, the sooner they'll make sales and the better their relationships will be with clients. Translation: They'll get more repeat and referral business. *Wahoo!!!*

What This Means to Your Sales Coaching

As mentioned earlier, your sales coaching approach will be slightly different when you are preventing this sales mistake. This is due to the past patterns and future anticipations required for preventing this sales mistake.

Notice in this set of sample sales coaching questions that the session doesn't start with asking about a specific sales conversation, but rather with discovering a pattern from the week before.

Here are some sample sales coaching questions you could use to deal with the sales mistake of being ill-prepared.

Sales Coaching Questions for Mistake #5

"Over the last week, which kinds of objections have you gotten the most of?"

"How many prospects had that type of objection this past week?"

"Do you normally get this many about this or is it something new?"

"What do you think that's about?"

"Is there any underlying reason to this objection? Is this objection connected to anything else going on?"

"If you had this objection, what would you want to know?"

"What are our competitors not telling clients that relates to this objection?"

"How can you position this objection as an advantage to clients?"

"What can you do to position this objection as an opportunity for someone who is shopping around?"

"How can you use the objection as a differentiator?"

"How are we a better option than our competitor?"

"How can you use the objection to demonstrate our integrity and trust-worthiness?"

"Let's brainstorm as many ways as possible for you to say that."

"Which way of saying it feels most natural to you?"

"How about you write that down then we'll put it in context in a role-play?"

"You want to read it to me?"

"What do you think? Does it feel like you?"

"How could you tweak it so it sounds more like you?"

"Great. Are you ready to role-play?" (*Let's say your team member says yes, the role-play is complete and he did a great job.*)

"Ready to use your new approach with real clients this next week?"

"Excellent. Let's touch base later next week to see how things are going for you with your new approach. What time on Thursday would work for you?"

Planning Preparation

Preparation with the following worksheet will get your team members helping their clients more effectively. You can receive a printable version of it at www.CoachingandSalesInstitute.com.

Have your team members fill out this chart over a week, couple of weeks, or month. Be sure to have them put in one topic in the left section of each column and then in the right section indicate the number of times that topic occurred. From this, you'll be able to analyze your team members' patterns from the past, and together you can better anticipate and prepare for their future sales interactions.

In this example, the results are from one of your team members this last week:

Column 1		Column 2		Column 3		Column 4		Column 5	
Client Objections		Client Questions		Client Information Requests		Information Looked Up		Social Media Research	
Setup fees	llll llll	Delivery	IIII	New version	IIII			Our new version and competition's new release	99+
		Release date of new version	IIII IIII IIII						

Based on the way your team member filled out the chart, together you can prioritize coaching sessions to help him be prepared to compare the new version of your product to the competition's new release. From this, you and your team members will know what they need to do to be better prepared.

As you coach your sales team members to prevent the sales mistake of being ill-prepared, focus on both the patterns of the past and the things they can anticipate happening in the future. By having both a past and future focus, you will ensure your team sells better, sooner, and more often.

Action Items from This Chapter

1. Coach your team members to practice and prepare for their sales conversations.

2. Take a no-excuses approach to your team's preparation.

3. Help your team be relationship focused.

4. Avoid responses that sound stiff and scripted.

5. Use the different coaching structure to help your team be better prepared.

6. Get your team members to share their opinions appropriately.

7. Facilitate your team's practice of answering clients' frequently asked questions.

8. Have your team respond to objections in a more helpful way.

9. Challenge your team to provide clients with the information they want.

10. Encourage your team to leverage technology to better understand what clients want.

CHAPTER 7

Sales Mistake #6

Taking Too Much of the Client's Time

Picture this: You're the executor for a close family member's will. You're responsible for dividing the estate assets among the family, and you want to ensure that everything is done fairly and respects any and all regulations.

You call the financial institution that holds the stock investments to book an appointment. The receptionist says to come in any time that's convenient for you.

You go to the financial institution and wait to meet with a financial advisor. You wait and wait. As you wait, you read over their marketing materials (because you're thinking about changing financial institutions). Finally, someone comes to meet you. She shakes your hand saying, "I'm so sorry to hear about your loss. My name is Carmen, and I'll help you with what you need to do."

You let Carmen know you have half an hour before you have to leave for an appointment. So you get right down to business. You explain you want to divide the stock assets among the family members and provide them all in kind (you had done your homework so you know the right term to use to explain that you don't want to cash out the stocks but you want to transfer them as they are).

Carmen, to your surprise and confusion, explains at length that you have to cash out the stocks to distribute them among the family members. You ask questions for clarity and remind her you have 15 minutes left. Again, Carmen goes on at length explaining the process involved.

Since you are not willing to accept Carmen's advice, you ask her to go speak with her boss about what she is suggesting. She's obviously not too happy about the idea but she leaves the room. She comes back and says, "Yes, my boss says we must cash them out."

Shocked again, you ask Carmen if there is a senior advisor whom you could speak to, and you add, "Carmen, I have less than five minutes left." You wonder, to yourself, if Carmen actually spoke with her boss. (This is a true story, believe it or not. It happened to me.)

Carmen leaves the room. She returns, takes you to another office, and introduces you to Janet, the senior financial advisor. You have three minutes left before you have to leave.

Janet asks you one question, "How much time do you have?"

You like Janet already. You say you have only five minutes because of an appointment.

You quickly explain the situation to Janet. You don't bother with the history of Carmen and her boss. Based on your time factor, you just go for the essentials. You explain you want to transfer the stock investments in kind rather than cash them out.

Janet's response: "Of course. All I need are the names of the individuals and their contact details. Once I have that, it'll take me 5 to 10 minutes to process the paperwork, which I can do once you are gone. I'll send you off an e-mail this morning once it's complete—that way we can get you out the door in time for your next appointment."

You provide Janet with the details and you are on your way in five minutes. You are a bit late because of Carmen, but Janet was helpful and quick. *Thank goodness.*

Janet handled the situation well in 5 minutes, whereas Carmen took more than 25 minutes to potentially really mess up the situation. And if you hadn't taken the initiative to ask questions, you would have been really late and your family members would have lost thousands of dollars. *Not good on Carmen's part.*

Are your team members acting more like Carmen or Janet with their prospects?

Carmen failed to heed my warnings about time constraints, and because of this she clearly committed the sales mistake of taking too much of the client's time.

This mistake is pervasive. Almost every salesperson has committed this mistake at one point or another, and most sales managers have no clue as to who on their teams are the perpetrators.

The good news is: It is one of the easiest sales mistakes to prevent. You can help your team eliminate the possibility of committing this mistake by including time in your sales coaching.

Sales Mistake Report Form

The Offender/Perpetrator – Enter the name of the company.

> *ABC Financial Institution, salesperson Carmen.*

Sales Mistake Committed – Identify the mistake made.

> - *Taking too much of the client's time.*
> - *Being ill-prepared.*

Your Statement – Clearly state the facts of what happened.

> - *The salesperson didn't demonstrate she heard the prospect's time restrictions.*
> - *The salesperson would have taken more of the prospect's time if she had allowed it.*

Evidence – Indicate what you wanted to buy but didn't.

> - *Financial services*

Future Potential Business – Outline what future business you represented.

> *Me, directly: I would represent one client to the financial institution.*
> *My friends and family members who live locally would represent even more potential clients.*

Do you include a time factor in your sales coaching? Do you know if your team members are clarifying how much time clients have? Are your team members able to communicate using stories, questions, and information of varying lengths of time?

Here's the Problem

If your team members don't clarify the time clients have for their conversations, they'll waste clients' time, lose the goodwill they created, and miss opportunities to make sales (as Carmen did with me).

If your team members have only one way of communicating, their sales conversations will always take a similar length of time and they'll miss out on sales opportunities, meaning they'll get fewer sales.

If your team members can't adapt their sales conversations to the time frames clients have, they'll get the reputation of not being client-focused and, consequently, get fewer referrals.

Bottom line: This sales mistake affects the goodwill your team members develop, their sales ratios, and the number of referrals they receive.

The Forensic Evidence

The following forensic evidence includes some of the clues left behind when Sales Mistake #6: Taking Too Much of Client's Time, is committed. Use the forensic evidence as a guideline to help you in your sales mistake detection, prevention, and rehabilitation.

Sales Numbers and Statistics – The potential statistical evidence you would notice about the perpetrators and their results.

> *Fewer sales meetings/conversations than other team members.*
> *Conversations take longer than other team members.*
> *Prospects don't book as many second appointments with perpetrating team member.*
> *Few to no referrals.*

Observable Prospect/Client Behavior – The potential evidence of the perpetrator's prospects and clients.

> *Prospects end conversations abruptly.*
> *Prospects can lose patience and get irritated.*
> *Prospects and clients explain they are too busy for a second meeting or conversation.*

Observable Team Member Behavior – The potential evidence the perpetrator exhibits in general.

Likes to talk.
    Can't seem to direct a conversation.
    Can be very charismatic.
    Demonstrates a lack of awareness of others' conversation cues.
    Has difficulties getting second meetings.
    Truly believes prospects are too busy for follow-up sales interactions.
    May process thoughts out loud (be very verbal).

Observable Coaching Behavior – The potential evidence the perpetrator exhibits in coaching sessions.

Talks more than other team members.
    Coaching sessions usually take longer to accomplish the same outcome.
    Complains about how busy prospects and clients are.
    Has difficulty staying on track.

What to Watch and Listen for in Your Sales Coaching

There are many expressions about the value of time, each demonstrating a different perspective of time's value:

"Time is a gift."

"Time is limited."

"Time is what you give to those you care about."

"Managing your time wisely is important."

"Prioritizing your time is essential."

"Don't waste time."

"Time is money."

The value of time is individual. Thus, the reason it is so important to sales. It's another element of the sales conversation that needs to be adapted to each individual client. It's part of your team members' customization to their clients' needs. There is no standard right length of time to help clients with their buying decisions. The right length of time is measured by the individual.

Direct your sales coaching based on the importance of being time adaptive in sales conversations. You'll want to coach your team members on how they use time in their sales interactions.

You'll notice your perpetrating team members may be guilty of doing any one, some or all of the following:

- Ignoring client feedback about time.
- Being unable to vary the length of what they say or ask.
- Providing little to no choice to clients.
- Being too open-ended in their questions.
- Not managing clients' time expectations well.

Get your team members to include time in their sales conversations for the next four weeks and see what happens to their sales. Your rehabilitated team members will see their sales and the number of their referrals increase.

Another Important Component

When coaching your team members, you want to help them become more aware of when they are losing clients' interest. This should be a clue for your team members to adapt better to clients and to shift their use of their clients' time.

To increase your team members' awareness of when client interest is declining, ask them questions. Have them reflect on what happened in their specific sales conversations, and revisit their interactions from the perspective client interest. This lens will help your team make fewer time blunders so they don't commit this mistake as Carmen did with me.

1. Demonstrating They Hear Client Feedback

The title of this section is not "Hearing Client Feedback"; it's "*Demonstrating They Hear Client Feedback*." The important word is *demonstrating*.

I'm sure Carmen heard what I said about my time frame, but she didn't demonstrate she heard me. If she had, I wouldn't have had to mention we were at the five-minute mark.

When you are coaching your team members to prevent this sales mistake, do ask about what they heard and what the client said but put the emphasis on how they demonstrated they heard what the client said.

Encourage your team to develop habits that are sensitive to client time concerns. For example, when setting up a meeting (whether in person, on the phone, or via some other technology), do your team members clarify how much time the meeting will take, including the items clients expect to be on the agenda? Do your team members check in with clients at the beginning of meetings to review if the time frames are still what they had planned or if there have been some changes? Do your team members follow an agenda and give time to wrap up the conversation with next steps?

These kinds of time-respecting behaviors will help your team members demonstrate they are hearing what clients have to say about their time frames. This will also remind them of the time sensitive-information that is important to clients.

2. Adapting to the Time Clients Have

As you know, you want your team members to be able to adapt the length of their sales conversations to the amount of time clients have.

Many managers ask me how they can get their team members to do this. You can help your team members be more time adaptable by including time in your sales coaching or their sales preparation. Even better, do it both ways. Get your team members to prepare and practice using the three different time versions of what they say to clients:

1. A bottom-line version in case the client is on the way out the door. (This is the version Janet used with me.)
2. A short version for clients who don't want a lot of detail.
3. Their regular version. The first two versions can sometimes become openers for more in-depth conversations. With these two, if clients are interested, they will ask for more detail, or ask to schedule time to hear something more like the third, full version.

By coaching your team members to provide you with shorter versions of what they normally say, you'll get to both the bottom-line and the short version. To get them moving in the right direction, you can ask questions to help them whittle down the length of what they say. For example:

- How about you say that in half the time?
- What are the essential parts of what you said?
- What would be the one-minute version of what you just said? (Short version)
- What would be the 30-second version of what you just said? (Bottom-line version)

On occasion, you'll have team members who don't provide enough detail. If this is the case, you will ask questions in the reverse, incrementally building from their shorter versions to longer ones.

Use this varied-length approach in your sales coaching to help your team members make better use of their time with clients.

3. Providing Clients with Choice

Encourage your team members to provide clients with choices in their sales conversations. Giving clients choices will ensure their interest stays high while making the best use of their time as well.

By providing clients with choices, you also give them control of the conversation, which will help your team members develop additional goodwill. This goodwill will build trust and put your team in a better position to help clients with their buying decisions.

By getting your team to focus on providing choices (and having clients feel more in control of their conversations), clients will get that your team is working *with* them. Your team members may provide clients with choices with questions such as:

"We have 10 minutes left. What would you be most interested in? Covering _____ or chatting about _____?"

"We have 30 minutes. We could begin with _____, _____, or _____. Where would you like to start?"

"We have three more things to cover based on what we planned. What order would you like to go in?"

"We have three things on our agenda . . . _____, _____, and _____. Which ones or one are priorities for you?"

You get the picture. Your team members would ask clients to pick what's most important to them in the time frame they have.

As you see, you can coach your team to ask clients about the types of choices including:

- Priority
- Interest level
- Order
- Importance

Salespeople are often surprised to discover clients don't need a lot of information about products to make their buying decisions. Clients just need enough of the *right* information for them to make their decision to buy. By including choices in your sales coaching, you'll ensure your team is providing enough of the right information, while also demonstrating that they respect and value the client's time.

4. Being Specific with Clients

So far we have focused on getting your team members to be more time effective in what they say. Yet clients can sometimes be the culprits behind too-long sales interactions. Sometimes they can go off on a tangent or ramble on about something that's unimportant or unrelated to the sale at hand.

You can help your team manage clients' effects on the length of sales conversations by asking your salespeople about the specific sales questions that seem to have taken the conversation off track. If your team members are like most, you will discover they asked an open-ended question that caused the client to ramble. While open-ended questions can be helpful to sales conversations, if the questions are not specific enough, they can cause clients to talk aimlessly.

When you are sales coaching and discover that a team member used an open-ended question that caused a client to ramble, ask him to brainstorm some alternative sales questions that are more specific, and more likely to provide the client with more direction.

For example, an open-ended question like "What happened?" may cause clients to ramble, but a question like "What specifically happened that caused the malfunction?" is more specific and would give the client more direction.

Sometimes the overgeneralized sales philosophy of using open-ended questions can be detrimental to the length of your team members' sales conversations. Encourage and coach your team to ask more specific open-ended questions that will solicit the kind of information they need to help clients with their buying decisions without taking too much time.

5. Managing Clients' Time Expectations

It's common for salespeople not to tell clients how long the sales process will typically take because they are concerned it will cause them not to buy. As you know, if your team members take too much of their clients' time, clients are less likely to buy, give referrals, and do repeat business. So sharing with clients how much time the sales process will take is essential to managing clients' time expectations.

What does this mean to your sales coaching?

It means you'll want to help your team members better communicate the time factor in their sales processes. Janet did a great job of letting me know how much time it would take to transfer the stock investments in kind, and she did it in such a way that it was a benefit to me (getting me out the door in time for my next appointment). She also shared when she would let me know the process was complete. Janet communicated the time factors well, and therefore managed my time expectations in a positive way.

When you're coaching your team members, ask them how they communicated the time factors involved in completing the sale, and the benefits of those time factors to the client. By asking these kinds of questions, you'll ensure your team members do a better job of managing clients' time expectations.

Get Really Practical

You'll want to get really practical in your sales coaching with your team members at times. This will help them develop great time habits.

During your sales coaching, inquire about the specifics of their sales interactions. For example, ask them how they keep track of time during their meetings. Ask how they clarify the agenda with clients. Ask who monitors the time. Ask how they divide their meeting time. Ask how they involve clients in these decisions. Simply by asking these kinds of practical questions, your team members will be more proactive with their use of clients' time. Your sales coaching is a simple way to improve your team members' management of client time in their sales conversations.

Meeting Idea for You

During a meeting with your team members, consider brainstorming what they can do to demonstrate they respect clients' time. Get them to look at what they can do before, during, and after a meeting.

Let me give you a personal-shopping example. Contrast the salesperson's actions in the following example with what Carmen did with me. You'll notice Susie, the salesperson, saves me shopping time as well as trying-on time. Here's a typical phone message Susie leaves for me every spring and fall:

> Hey, Peri! Susie here. I hope you are doing well. We just got in your favorite suit designer. We'll have the line out on the floor tomorrow. If you can, call me 15 minutes before you come in and I'll pull some pieces for you and have them ready in the changing room.

Talk about respecting my time!

You may be thinking that Susie can do this because she works at a high-end shop. No, she works at a great discount business clothier. Susie really demonstrates she respects my time, and in a big city like Toronto (the fifth largest in North America), I have a lot of choices, but because of Susie's respect for my time, I'm loyal to Tom's Place.

What can your team members do to demonstrate they respect how important time is to clients?

What This Means to Your Sales Coaching

Your sales coaching questions can help your team members demonstrate they respect their clients' time. Listen to your team members and discover what is working for them, and what is not.

Here are some sample sales coaching questions you could use to prevent the mistake of taking too much of the client's time.

Sales Coaching Questions for Sales Mistake #6

"Sounds like a great meeting. How long was it?"

"How long were the clients expecting the meeting to be?"

"How do we know that's what they expected?"

"What did you say or ask to clarify the length of time you would need for the meeting?"

"What did they say to indicate what time frame would work?"

"Did you get a chance to check in at the beginning of your meeting to see if the planned meeting time was still good?"

"Were there any changes in the length of time they had for the meeting?"

"Did you get a chance to cover everything *you* thought was important in the meeting?"

"Did you get a chance to cover everything that was important to *them* in the meeting?"

"How do you know?"

"What did they say was important to them that you covered in the meeting?"

"What did they agree to have covered in the meeting?"

"Were there parts of the meeting that felt more rushed than the other parts?"

"What parts of the conversation did they seem more interested in?"

"What were you talking about then?"

"What parts of the conversation did they seem less interested in?"

"What were you talking about at those points?"

"Did you get a chance to provide some choices of where the conversation could have gone from there?"

"What choices could you have given at that point?"

"Were you giving the bottom-line, short, or regular version when interest seemed to go down?" *(Let's say your team member said regular version.)*

"Do you know if that was the version they wanted?"

"What could you have asked to clarify which version they wanted?"

"What is your bottom-line version?"

"What is your short version?"

"What are you going to do next time a client's interest seems to wane?" *(Your team member is going to ask which version the client would prefer.)*

"What are you going to ask?"

"I like your approach. How about you give it a try for the next week and we touch base with one another to see how it goes? What morning of the following week works for you for us to touch base?"

Time-Adaptive Preparation

Thorough sales preparation is a great strategy to prevent your team members taking up too much of their clients' time. Use the following exercise to help your team members be more time adaptive. You can receive a printable version of it at www.CoachingandSalesInstitute.com.

For each product, fill out this chart.

Product _____

Column 1	Column 2	Column 3	Column 4
Write out what you typically say about this product.	Write out the bottom-line version of what you wrote in Column 1.	Write out the short version of what you wrote in Column 1.	What could you ask a client to see which version they would prefer?

This chart will help your team members develop different versions of what they say to clients. It will force them to come up with a variety of lengths of what they usually say. They'll also learn what questions to ask so clients can guide the allocation of meeting time.

As you coach your team members to prevent taking too much of their clients' time, get them to demonstrate that they heard clients' feedback, adapted to time frames, provided choices, asked specific questions, and managed time expectations. These five elements will ensure your team is rehabilitated. Clients will be grateful for your team's respect of their time, and as an added bonus, you will likely gain more repeat business and referrals.

Action Items from This Chapter

1. Encourage your team members to be time-adaptive with clients.

2. Include time in your sales coaching sessions for the next four weeks as a test.

3. Get your team members to notice and measure clients' interest levels.

4. Have your team members demonstrate they hear clients' time feedback.

5. Encourage time-respecting behaviors with clients.

6. Help your team develop and practice bottom-line, short, and regular versions of what they say.

7. Coach your team members to provide clients with choice.

8. Ask targeted questions to reduce clients' tendency to ramble.

9. Teach your team members to better manage clients' time expectations.

10. Work with your team members to develop and communicate good time habits.

CHAPTER 8

Sales Mistake #7

Sharing What's Not Relevant

Picture this: You're part of a committee selecting a hotel for a conference of 400 of your peers. You want the hotel to be a fitting choice. You want it to be memorable (for good reasons, not bad ones), and you want to ensure everyone will be treated well.

You arrive in the city where the conference is going to be held, ready to visit the five hotels on the committee's short list. You and the other committee members have finished the property visits to the first four hotels, and all four have potential. The staffs were helpful, the service was outstanding, and the food was delicious. But two properties really stood out because they met the committee's essential decision-making criteria. These two properties have rooms you could expand to accommodate potential additional attendees, and both have all their meeting rooms on one floor so it'll be easier for your peers to navigate.

You and the other committee members are looking forward to seeing the fifth hotel. You all arrive and wait to meet with their salesperson, Bernard. And you wait. You try to reach Bernard on his cell, with no luck, so you all continue to wait.

Bernard finally arrives, looking as if he dropped his papers somewhere. He has a file with your conference name on it, but it has papers sticking out in all directions. It is a sign of what's to come.

Personally, you're rooting for Bernard's hotel since you love the location and you know his hotel chain has a reputation for great service. All he has to do is meet the committee's room requirements and it'll be a done deal. *Go, Bernard!*

While Bernard begins to show you around the property, he gets lost. *Not a good sign.* He then gets back on track and finds the meeting room that he has listed as best suited for your group—but it doesn't meet the committee's minimum occupancy requirements.

You're probably thinking that Bernard must be new on the job. The sad news is that he has been in the hospitality business for over a decade and he is the senior salesperson at his hotel. You think to yourself, "Aren't we glad we didn't get their junior salesperson!"

It gets worse, though. He goes on to show you the breakout rooms, which are on three different floors. Bernard failed to meet two of your committee's top priorities. Both are deal breakers for you and the other committee members.

Boy, did Bernard miss the mark and share what wasn't relevant! He would have been better not to show the rooms. Because of his actions, all the committee members dismiss Bernard's hotel, and they aren't even willing to give Bernard a second chance to show them other rooms that suit their needs. His goodwill with the committee members is gone because he showed them product that isn't relevant to their needs. The committee members are done with Bernard and his hotel.

Bernard clearly demonstrated he didn't know what was relevant for the committee members, even though they had laid out their needs concisely both verbally and in written documents.

Sales Mistake Report Form

The Offender/Perpetrator – Enter the name of the company.

ABC Hotel, salesperson Bernard.

Sales Mistake Committed – Identify the mistake made.

Sharing what's not relevant.

Your Statement – Clearly state the facts of what happened.

- *The salesperson didn't review what the prospects wanted.*
- *The salesperson showed prospects product that wasn't relevant to their needs.*

Evidence – Indicate what you wanted to buy but didn't.

Hotel contract for 400 for 4 days.

Future Potential Business – Outline what future business you represented.

You and the committee members would directly represent this conference of 400 people, and future conferences. (The committee is a repeat customer of hotels in another conference city because the salesperson there showed them relevant offerings.)

Your peers who attended the conference would represent even more business.

Bernard's lack of attention to what was important to the committee is a prime example of the sales mistake of sharing what's not relevant.

Sometimes this mistake is committed by salespeople because they have bought into the philosophy of selling what's on the shelf. The problem in today's marketplace is that clients don't want to buy based on what *you have*. They want to buy based on what *they want and need*.

Clients don't want instant gratification alone. They want customization; they want to buy from the company that will give them what they want on their terms—not a company that sells on its own terms.

When your team members share what's not relevant, they demonstrate that they don't hear clients. Your team members are sending the message that clients are not worth listening to. From a client perspective, your perpetrating team members imply that they don't care enough to earn their business.

Here's the Problem

If your team members don't really listen, they'll miss what is important to clients. Without hearing clients' needs, they'll talk about stuff that's not important or relevant, and they'll lose sales (as Bernard did).

If your team members don't share what's relevant to clients, they'll come across as incompetent, and clients will refuse to give them a second chance (as the committee did with Bernard).

Simply put, this sales mistake prevents your team from even entering the sales arena. If your team members are committing this mistake, they are shooting themselves in the sales foot. It's the quickest way for your team members to lose goodwill, credibility, and sales.

The Forensic Evidence

The following forensic evidence includes some of the clues left behind when Sales Mistake #7, Sharing What's Not Relevant, is committed. Use the forensic evidence as a guideline to help you in your mistake detection, prevention, and rehabilitation.

Sales Numbers and Statistics – The potential statistical evidence you would notice about the perpetrator or results of the perpetrator of this sales mistake.

- *Conversations are shorter.*
- *Not much repeat business.*
- *Low sales.*
- *Longer to close sales.*
- *Few, if any, referrals.*

Observable Prospect/Client Behavior – The potential evidence of the perpetrator's prospects and clients.

- *Seem to disappear.*
- *Ask for more information in other ways.*
- *Clients ask a lot of questions about agenda of next meeting before agreeing to meet.*

Observable Team Member Behavior – The potential evidence the perpetrator exhibits in general.

- *Demonstrates poor listening skills.*
- *Doesn't consistently ask good questions.*
- *Tries to fit what's available to the clients' needs, rather than starting with the clients' needs and trying to meet them.*
- *May be an advocate of the sell-what's-on-the-shelf philosophy.*

Observable Coaching Behavior – The potential evidence the perpetrator exhibits in coaching sessions.

- *Bases what is important to clients on available product(s), not on clients' needs.*
- *Can't explain clients' needs.*

What to Watch and Listen for in Your Sales Coaching

As Bernard clearly demonstrated, sales can be made or broken depending on how relevant the salesperson's offerings are. If what clients are shown is not relevant, the sale is usually lost. This is the unfortunate by-product of the sales mistake of sharing what's not relevant.

Relevancy is essential to good salesmanship. Yet, how often have you, as a client, experienced a salesperson trying to sell you something that isn't relevant to your expressed needs or desires? If you are like most people, it's happened too often.

If you're like most sales managers, you're probably not sure who on your team are the perpetrators of this sales mistake.

There are three ways you can tell if your team members are sharing what's not relevant. They include:

1. Not listening well to clients' needs.

2. Not determining clients' belief or understanding issue.

3. Providing irrelevant information.

You can help your team members be more relevant to their clients by noticing these three signs and taking action in your sales coaching to prevent them.

1. Really Listening

As I shared earlier in this book, listening is a *feeling*, yet, many mistake listening as only a skill.

Part of your responsibility with your team members is to help them really understand that good listening depends on how they make clients *feel*. If you put the emphasis on listening as a skill only, your team members will focus on what *they* themselves do. If your team members perceive listening as a feeling, they will center their attention on *clients*. With this approach, your team members will measure their listening success on if and how much clients felt listened to during their sales interactions.

This adds a new dimension to your sales coaching. It puts attention on the specifics of what clients actually said, rather than on your team members' interpretation of what was said. This slight shift in your coaching will make a huge difference to how relevant your team members will be to their clients. No longer will your sales coaching sessions be about misinterpretations of clients' priorities, but rather about the specifics of what clients *said* was important to them.

Also, help your team members be even more relevant by encouraging them to check with clients to make sure what they heard was accurate. When checking in with clients, your rehabilitated team members may say something like:

"I just want to check in and make sure my understanding is correct . . ."

"Correct me if I'm wrong. You want _____ and you're concerned about _____. Is that right?"

Imagine how different the committee's visit to Bernard's hotel would have been if he had just done this before he started to show you the meeting rooms. If your team members don't listen well, they can mess up the conversation that comes afterward (as Bernard did).

By getting your team members to reflect on what they heard, you ensure they are on the right track before they move on to the next step. It ensures what they say is relevant to their clients.

You'll find it helpful to get your team members engaged in activities to improve their listening. For example, you could use your sales meetings as an opportunity to develop your team's listening. Whenever someone demonstrates poor listening skills, they could put money into a pot for a charitable donation or an office pizza party. Be creative and get your team members involved in how they can make giving one another feedback about their listening fun and engaging. The key is to get your team members more actively demonstrating, practicing, and developing their listening.

2. Providing Belief or Understanding

This topic will fine-tune your team members' sales processes, but it bears sharing. I'm surprised how often salespeople go on and on, presenting information that is not important to clients.

Adding the following to your sales coaching will prevent your team members from causing their clients to glaze over from information overload or disinterest. It amounts to only a few questions, but these questions will help your team members come up with more relevant responses to client feedback.

Here's how it works: Ask your perpetrating team members if clients are less likely to believe or understand the information they share. This simple determination will help your team members decide what to say next to make sure it is most relevant to the clients' needs.

If your team members determine clients are *less likely to believe*, they would then provide supporting information to prove their point. This may include:

- Facts, figures, and numbers
- Independent research
- Reviews
- Comparison charts
- Income projections

Ensure your team members have access to this kind of factual information to help clients shift their beliefs.

If your team members determine clients are *less likely to understand*, they would share supporting information that demonstrates what they are going to say. This could involve:

- Explanation of product in action
- A client success story (for more on these, see Chapter 3)
- A demonstration of the product
- A step-by-step explanation
- An analogy
- Some client testimonials

During your coaching sessions, help your team members determine which supporting material will work best with which products or features for clients who are less likely to understand.

This determination of whether or not the client will be less likely to believe or understand what your team members are going to say about your product will help them provide the most appropriate and relevant information for their clients.

We'll pull this all together in just a moment.

3. Providing Relevant Information

For the sake of illustration, let's say you are coaching one of your perpetrating team members, Diana. She is preparing for a sales conversation, and has listened to her client, George, to determine the ABC widget best suits his needs. Diana's also figured out what George is less likely to believe and understand about the widget. Diana is ready to practice putting it all together to provide the most relevant information for her client.

Diana discovered George is concerned about the time and money it will take to install the widget. Diana determined that the time it takes to install is probably something George is less likely to understand, while the costs involved for the ABC widget are probably something he is less likely to believe.

So Diana decides when she speaks about the installation time for the widget, she will share a client success story, and some testimonial videos of how the company either met or surpassed the client's expected time frames. This information will help George better understand the details of the installation time frames.

Diana also chooses to support her discussion with a breakdown of the costs if George gets the widget now compared to one year from now. This way George can see how much money he saves on repair costs in the year, and how quickly he makes his investment back by getting the widget today. This information will get him to believe the benefits of buying the widget now.

If you coach your team members to do this kind of matching, their sales conversations will come together like a beautiful puzzle. It will feel like great customization to clients. Practice this "less likely to believe" and "less likely to understand" way of providing information with your team members to make it appear effortless to clients, and eventually it will feel effortless for salespeople.

What This Means to Your Sales Coaching

Your sales coaching questions will help your team members provide more relevant information for their clients, and put you in the position to listen to what is going on.

Here are some sample sales coaching questions you could use to deal with the sales mistake of sharing what's not relevant.

Sales Coaching Questions for Sales Mistake #7

"What were the client's top criteria for making the buying decision?"

"What did they specifically say about the top criteria?"

"What did they say was most important?"

"What did they say were deal breakers?"

"What did they say were nice-to-haves?"

"What did you do to demonstrate you heard what they said?"

"What did you say to check that what you heard was accurate?" (*Let's say your team member didn't check in with the client.*)

"What could you have said to check that what you heard was accurate?"

"What information would they need to know about our product based on what they said was important to them?"

"Would they be less likely to believe or less likely to understand that information?" (*Let's say your team member said less likely to believe.*)

"Based on that, what kind of supporting information would be most helpful to provide?" (*Let's say your team member doesn't know.*)

"What options can you think of that would provide the proof that would be helpful?"

"How about we brainstorm some more options?"

"What about some independent reviews?"

"Primary or secondary research?"

"Comparison chart?"

"What about a cost analysis, like the one you did for Mr. Jones last month?"

"Which one(s) do you think would have suit this client's needs best?"

"Makes sense to me. How about you put it all together? What would it sound like?"

"I like it. Could you use this kind of supporting information in your other sales interactions?" (*Let's say the answer is yes and your team member describes the other ways to use it.*)

"How about this? Use the supporting information where appropriate this coming week and then let's touch base to see how it's working for you. Maybe we can do some polishing of how you use it then, or we can move on to other things. Work for you?"

"When would you like to touch base?"

Relevancy Preparation

As you know, the better prepared your team members are at sharing what is relevant to their clients, the more likely they will sell more. Have them fill out this chart based on a week's sales activity or on specific sales conversations that didn't go as well as they would like.

You can receive a printable version of it at www.CoachingandSalesInstitute.com.

Column 1	Column 2	Column 3	Column 4	Column 5	Column 6
List each of the clients you had a sales conversation with.	What did you hear the client say about what was important to him/her?	Did you check with the client that what you heard was accurate?	Was your client less likely to believe or less likely to understand what you were going to share about our product?	What possible information could you have shared with your client (that matches what you wrote in Column 4)?	What supporting information would have been the most relevant for that client?

This chart will help your team members become more aware of:

- What they are doing to demonstrate they're listening.
- Whether clients are less likely to believe or less likely to understand what they're going to share about your product.
- How to share what is most relevant to clients.

They'll learn to better match what clients say they're interested in or concerned about to the information they share about your product.

By preventing this sales mistake, you put your team members back into the selling game, allowing them to develop the goodwill and credibility to sell. By continuing to help your perpetrating team members really listen, determine if clients are less likely to believe or understand, and match what they say to what clients want, you help them sell more.

Action Items from This Chapter

1. Help your team members recognize that listening is a feeling.

2. Get your team members checking with clients that their understanding is accurate.

3. Have your team members measure the success of their listening through their clients' eyes.

4. Coach your team members not by their interpretation of what clients said, but by using clients' words.

5. Engage your team members in activities to demonstrate, practice, and develop their listening.

6. Do the "less likely to believe" or "less likely to understand" test with your team members.

7. Assist your team members to discover the best factual information for clients who are less likely to believe.

8. Coach your team members to determine which explanatory information will work best for clients who are less likely to understand.

9. Help your team members practice providing information for clients who are less likely to believe or understand.

10. Promote team members' use of the relevancy sales preparation sheet.

CHAPTER

9

Sales Mistake #8

Missing Prospects' Buying Cues

We're house stalking. It's early spring and frost is on the ground. We sit in our car looking at yet another house in town with a "For Sale" sign on its lawn. My husband has finally decided he's ready to move. I'm excited.

We admire the house's design and stone exterior and speculate about how life would be different if we lived in the city. We chat about hiking the conservation park trails every morning before starting our days. We talk about walking to local restaurants for our weekly dates. We speak about being part of a community that we always thought we missed by living in the country. We're painting an enticing picture of what life would look like if we move. (As you know, prospects' imaginations are one of the most powerful sales tools available to your team members.)

Then another car drives up, and the lovely little picture we are creating dissolves. My husband playfully says, "Looks like we have competition." *We naively thought we were the only ones who house stalked.*

I should preface what is about to happen with this: At this point, we don't have a real estate agent. Up until now, we have just been looking online at which houses are available in town.

The other car sits there for the longest time. Then, finally, the door opens and out steps a gentleman in a well-tailored gray suit—polished and professional looking.

He walks over to our car on my husband's side and says, "Are you Mark?"
My husband says, "Nope," giving me a discreet wave not to say anything.
Gray Suit says, "Thanks," and promptly proceeds back to his car.

I'm about to call Gray Suit back to engage him in a conversation about the house, when my husband holds me back and says, "Let's see what he does."

We go back to creating our picture of living in town. Maybe we would get a dog. Maybe we would join some of the town's clubs. We continue for 10 minutes as we wait to see what Gray Suit does.

Gray Suit never speaks to us. Mark doesn't show. In fact, Gray Suit doesn't even look at us again, even when we leave (we drive away slowly in case he wants to get our attention). Not even a nod or a wave goodbye from Gray Suit.

Talk about missing the mark on many levels! (*Yes, pun intended.*)

Sales Mistake Report Form

The Offender/Perpetrator – Enter the name of the company.

> *ABC Real Estate Company, salesperson Gray Suit*

Sales Mistake Committed – Identify the mistake made.

> *Missing prospects' buying cues.*

Your Statement – Clearly state the facts of what happened.

- *The salesperson missed the prospects' buying cues (sitting out in the cold, admiring a house with a "For Sale" sign on it).*
- *The salesperson treated potential prospects as if they weren't there.*
- *The salesperson didn't even engage in a conversation.*

Evidence – Indicate what you wanted to buy but didn't.

> *A house.*

Future Potential Business – Outline what future business you represented.

- *Us directly: the commissions on our buying a new house and selling our current house.*
- *Our friends would represent even more business.*

Gray Suit's missing of the mark is a perfect example of the sales mistake of missing prospects' buying cues. He totally missed that we were interested in buying a house, that house. All he had to do was ask us a few questions to demonstrate his real-estate savvy and Gray Suit would probably have had us as new clients.

Talk about buying cues. We were sitting out in the cold admiring a house with a "For Sale" sign on it. I'm sure it would have been a dead giveaway to most real estate agents. I'm sure some wish to have the opportunity to run into buyers who are so interested.

If Gray Suit had only engaged us in a brief conversation and had asked a few questions, he would have quickly discovered the depth of our interest. *But alas . . . nothing.* Gray Suit knows nothing of our interest and nothing about us—and nothing about the friends we have who are also interested in buying in town.

Salespeople sometimes miss prospects' buying cues—often because they aren't always aware of what is going on around them. Sometimes it's because they are having a bad day, and other times because they just aren't conscious of the buying cues in their industry.

A classic exercise to illustrate this is to close your eyes (not yet, wait for the rest of the instructions) and count all the things in the room that you remember being red. Then, open your eyes and see how many red things there are. Now, close your eyes again and, in your mind's eye, count how many things are red.

So how many red objects are there in the room? And, without looking around, how many blue things are there?

My guess is you were more ready for how many red objects there were than you were for how many blue objects. Why? You probably took note of the number of red things when your eyes were open because you wanted to see how it affected your results, but you weren't focused on the blue things.

When salespeople commit this mistake, they have a similar experience. They may be so focused on specific things (red objects) that they miss out on prospects' buying cues (blue objects).

How often are your team members acting like Gray Suit and missing out on the buying cues of their future clients?

Here's the Problem

If your team members don't register prospects' buying cues, they'll miss opportunities to build relationships with prospects and to position themselves to help prospects with their buying decisions (as Gray Suit did with us).

Bluntly put, if your team members are missing prospects' buying cues, they *ain't* selling. They're missing opportunities to sell to prospects who are ready to buy (as Gray Suit did). They're missing opportunities to make sales in a short amount of time.

It would be like having a winning lottery ticket but not bothering to check the numbers. You may say your perpetrators of this sales mistake are sitting on free money.

The Forensic Evidence

The following forensic evidence includes some of the clues left behind when Sales Mistake #8, Missing Prospects' Buying Cues, is committed. Use the forensic evidence as a guideline to help you in your sales mistake detection, prevention, and rehabilitation.

Sales Numbers and Statistics – The potential statistical evidence you would notice about perpetrators and their results.

- *A lot of sales activity but not many sales.*
- *Low close ratio.*
- *Fewer prospects than non-perpetrating team members.*
- *Fewer clients than non-perpetrating team members.*

Observable Prospect/Client Behavior – The potential evidence of the perpetrator's prospects or clients.

- *Prospects who want to buy from your company ask to work with a different team member.*
- *Prospects buy from a competitor even though they were ready to buy when they met your perpetrator.*

Observable Team Member Behavior – The potential evidence the perpetrator exhibits in general.

- *Goes through the sales motions (e.g., networking, asking for referrals, etc.), but doesn't sell much.*
- *Will be in proximity with ripe prospects, but won't sell anything.*
- *Is busy but does not produce sales results.*

Observable Coaching Behavior – The potential evidence the perpetrator exhibits in coaching sessions.

- *Uses language like "should have" and "ought to have bought."*
- *Usually talks more than listens.*
- *Focuses on being right rather than on how to improve.*
- *Has low curiosity about people.*
- *Doesn't find it easy to answer your sales questions about what specifically a prospect did or said.*

What to Watch and Listen for in Your Sales Coaching

Almost every salesperson has a hidden fantasy of having prospects knocking down their door to buy their wares. Though this isn't a reality, prospects are often ready to buy, and salespeople miss the buying cues.

It's often tough for sales managers to know if their team members are missing prospects' buying cues. Think of Gray Suit's sales manager. He probably has no idea Gray Suit did what he did. He probably thought Gray Suit was out meeting Mark that day and nothing else happened. So don't be hard on yourself if you don't know if any of your team members are committing this mistake.

You may find it helpful to assume some of your team members are committing this sales mistake and, therefore, include some of the appropriate sales coaching questions in your coaching. The worst that can happen is you discover no one on your team is committing this sales mistake, but the best thing that could happen is that your team members' sales increase. Sounds like a reasonable risk to take, with no negative effects.

Your perpetrating team members will be guilty of:

1. Not noticing prospects' buying cues.

2. Not engaging prospects in conversations.

When you are watching and listening to detect this mistake, you'll want to be on the lookout for team members who do not notice people or details (including missing prospects' buying cues and not engaging prospects in conversations).

1. Noticing Buying Cues

The first step to your team members noticing prospects' buying cues is to increase their awareness of what happened in specific interactions. Reflect on Gray Suit's actions. He didn't even engage us in a conversation because he wasn't aware of our buying cues, but if his sales manager had helped him increase his awareness, he would certainly have engaged us in a sales conversation.

As the sales coach, get your team members going back in their minds to their sales conversations with prospects, then ask questions to help them become more aware of what was happening. Your questions help them notice the cues they didn't see before.

As you do this, your team members will begin to see things in a different light and will often realize how blind they had been. Try to keep them (and you) out of the judgment zone. It will only slow things down in your sales coaching process. Instead, focus on what they are noticing, and increase their awareness of one buying cue at a time.

To clarify, your sales coaching up to this point in the coaching session has been about prospects' behaviors, not about your team members' interpretation of those behaviors. And there has been no judgment of team members for not noticing earlier.

Once you've reached a point in your sales coaching session where your team members have noticed the prospects' buying behaviors in detail, ask about what those behaviors could mean. Brainstorm the possible alternative interpretations. Then, ask questions to focus on what are the most likely options. This will help your team members discover what most likely happened. This whole process will have your team members more effectively noticing prospects' buying cues.

An Added Piece

Every industry has its own set of prospect buying cues. Knowing this, engage your team members in brainstorming the buying cues in your industry. If your team members sell multiple products, have your team members brainstorm different buying cues for different products. Brainstorming about different products can help them cross-sell more effectively. And also consider brainstorming with your team members buying cues, that are time-specific—the ones they might notice before, during, and after a sale. All of these can be great topics for sales meetings or one-on-one coaching sessions.

As you coach your team members, they will increase their awareness to the point where they will be actively on the lookout for these prospect behaviors. Your team members will start to automatically notice and respond appropriately to prospects' buying cues related to the industry, various products, and timing.

Your team members can become awareness machines if you create the sales coaching dialogue to get them noticing buying cues.

Once your team members are aware of the buying cues they missed, you'll find that most of them will know what to do next. They'll be able to shift into responding appropriately to those buying cues.

2. Engaging Prospects in Conversations

Some sales managers feel it is unnecessary to mention in coaching conversations that salespeople should engage prospects, but experience indicates that salespeople don't always take such a proactive approach. It may seem like asking a fish to swim, but, think of Gray Suit and his actions.

Sometimes salespeople don't engage in conversations because they don't know what to say or do to start and keep conversations going. With this mind, you'll find it helpful to coach your team members on how to strike up a conversation with future clients in a way that is valuable to both parties. In your sales coaching, ask questions about what your team members could say and ask. As you know, you want them to be actively engaging prospects in such a way that gets prospects talking about themselves and sharing what's important to them.

Ask your team members how they can introduce themselves in a personal way. Also include in your sales coaching what your team members can ask to discover prospects' interest level, buying criteria, and need for help.

For example, Gray Suit could have introduced himself (so I could call him by his name and stop calling him Gray Suit). He could have asked for our business cards or given us his. He could have asked if we were looking for a house. He could have asked if we were interested in the particular house we were stalking. You get the picture. There are many directions Gray Suit could have taken the conversation.

The same is true for your perpetrating team members. They have many options when it comes to engaging their prospects in conversations. The more possibilities you help them see, the more likely they'll use one of those options with future clients. It's like cooking. If you only know how to cook one recipe and you don't have those ingredients in the cupboard, there's nothing to eat. But if you know how to cook ten recipes and you don't have the ingredients for that one recipe, you still have nine options left.

The more conversation recipes your team members have, the more likely they will be able to cook up some great sales conversations.

3. Motivating for Next Time

Here's a sale coaching secret for you. Your sales coaching strategy to prevent this sales mistake isn't complete yet. Why? Because it's all too easy for your team members to fall back into the old behaviors of not noticing prospects' buying cues, which will mean they won't engage in those conversations. Human behavior typically follows the easiest path.

So what's a sales coach to do? This is where you have your team members share the possibilities with you, and have them tell you what the business is worth. It's a simple two-step process.

First, have them share how many times they find themselves in a situation like the one you just coached them through. And second, have them calculate how much potential commission it would mean for them.

For example, with Gray Suit you would ask him how many times he's seen someone parked in a car outside a house with a "For Sale" sign. Then you would have him calculate the potential value of the commissions his missed opportunities represented. Presto, Gray Suit has just provided himself with his motivation for noticing prospects' buying cues next time.

If you really want to anchor his new learnings, you may want to ask him how he would spend those added commissions. Just like prospects' imaginations are a powerful sales tool, your team members' imaginations can be a great sales coaching tool.

What This Means to Your Sales Coaching

Your sales coaching questions are the fuel to put you in the position to listen to what is going on for your team members. Particularly with this mistake, you may find it difficult to refrain from saying what you're thinking. Many sales managers have shared with me that they would like to wring the necks of their perpetrating team members of this mistake. If you feel this way about the perpetrators on your team, focus on engaging your genuine curiosity as you ask your questions. Do what you are asking them to do: notice.

The following are some sample sales coaching questions you could use to eliminate the sales mistake of missing prospects' buying cues. For this example, we're going to coach Gray Suit.

Sales Coaching Questions for Sales Mistake #8

"Let's go back to the situation again. Tell me what you noticed when you drove up to the house?"

"How many people were in the car?"

"Were they two males, two females, or a male and female?"

"What were they doing?"

"Were they pointing at the house at all?"

"Did they look like they were arguing or discussing something?"

"If they were pointing to the house and talking about something, what could they have been talking about?"

"What else could they be talking about?"

"What were they most likely talking about?"

"When you approached the car, what did you say?"

"What did the man say in response?"

"What did you say after that?"

"What happened next?"

"Did you get a chance to introduce yourself?"

"Did you speak to the woman?"

"So if they were chatting about the house, what could you have said to engage in a conversation to find out if they were potential prospects?"

"What could you have done to introduce yourself?"

"What could you have asked to find out if they were interested in buying a house?"

"What could you have asked to figure out if they were interested in this particular house?"

"What could you have asked to measure their interest level?"

"What could you have asked to find out how clear their buying criteria were?"

"What could you have asked to discover their buying criteria?"

"What could you have asked to discover if they needed help?"

"What could you have said to find out if they had a real estate agent?"

"We've covered a lot of ground. What stands out for you from our discussion?" (*Let's say Gray Suit says he's never going to not engage in a conversation again.*)

"What are you going to do to ensure you don't miss an opportunity like this again?" (*Gray Suit responds, "Whenever I see a couple in a car, I'm going to introduce myself and engage in a conversation"*)

"How often do you see a couple looking at a house in a car?" (*Gray Suit says,* "*Once every two weeks.*")

"So potentially, how much extra business would that mean for you?" (*Gray Suit does a brief mental calculation and smiles.* "*That's a nice chunk of change.*")

"How about you use this new approach of introducing yourself and engaging in a conversation when you see someone in a car for the next few weeks and then we'll follow up with each another to see how it worked for you? What time frames would work for you this time next month?"

Buying Cue Preparation

The more aware your team members are, the less likely they will be to miss prospects' buying cues. You can help increase their awareness through reflection and practice.

Use the following exercise to prevent your team from committing this sales mistake. You can receive a printable version of it at www.CoachingandSalesInstitute .com.

Before your team members start, have them list the typical prospect buying cues specific to your industry and your products.

Next, have your team members reflect over their week and fill out this chart.

Column 1	Column 2	Column 3	Column 4	Column 5
List the people you spoke with today/this week.	Which buying cues did the person in Column 1 demonstrate?	Which buying cues did you respond to in your sales conversation with the prospect listed in Column 1?	Which buying cues did you not notice or respond to in your sales conversation with the prospect listed in Column 1?	What could you have asked or said when the prospect in Column 1 demonstrated the buying cues you listed in Column 4?

Filling out this chart will help your perpetrating team members become more aware of the buying cues in your industry, which will help them know what to ask and say to respond more appropriately to prospects who are eager and ready to buy. With your sales coaching and the application of the insights they gain by filling out this chart, they'll sell more often to their prospects and clients.

By preventing this sales mistake, you put your team in a better position to sell. To prevent missing prospect buying cues, increase your team's awareness of prospects' buying signs, their ability to start and keep conversations going, and their sales motivation. Your sales coaching will help rehabilitate your perpetrating team members and prevent this sales mistake from even existing on your team.

Action Items from This Chapter

1. Get your team members to notice buying cues.

2. Brainstorm the buying cues related to your industry, various products, and timing.

3. Coach your team members on how they can start conversations with prospects.

4. Encourage your team members to develop questions to keep their conversations going.

5. Have your team practice how to get prospects talking about themselves.

6. Practice introductions with your team members.

7. Rehearse what your team members can say about themselves.

8. Role-play how to start and keep conversations going with your team members.

9. Help your team members develop different ways to engage prospects in conversations.

10. Leverage your team members' imaginations to motivate them to stay focused on noticing buying cues.

CHAPTER 10

Sales Mistake #9

Acting like a Traditional Salesperson

I t's that time of year: conference time. I have been going religiously for 14 years, and this year would be no different. Most of the decisions about going are no-brainers. Book my spot for the conference. *Check.* Book my flight to get there. *Check.* Book my hotel room for the 6 days . . .

Word amongst my colleagues is we can get the room at a lower rate if we do a pay-in-advance option. I can do that. After all, in 14 years (amidst illness, family, and business commitments), I haven't missed a single conference. So it's pretty safe to guess I would be there this year.

I get the details from one of my colleagues. If I book the hotel and pay in advance, my room will be $150 per night versus the regular $279 per night. I'll save over $600 if I pay in advance. It feels reasonable to pay in full and take the non-refundable risk, so I call the hotel. Caroline answers with her warm southern accent.

I check with her that indeed my colleagues' pay-in-advance information is accurate. Caroline confirms that they are correct.

Caroline then says, "Would you like to go ahead and book it?"

I respond, "Yes. Let's make this happen."

Caroline walks me through the choices. She gets down to the choice of two queens or a king. Caroline says, "The king will be $289 and the two queens will be $279. Which do you prefer, the king or the two queens?" Then she goes oddly quiet.

Caroline just tried to close me on something I don't want to buy. She is trying to get me to make a buying decision before she even gets what I want on the table. It feels like she is rushing me. And what she is trying to sell me was more expensive. *Ouch.*

Does Caroline think I forgot about the pay-in-advance option? Has Caroline forgotten about that option? Or is Caroline going for the close without any apparent concern about what I want?

Caroline's warm southern accent now feels like a put-on. I feel she is trying to take advantage of me. (*I doubt that was her intent, but it certainly felt that way.*) So, I ask Caroline about the pay-in-advance option. I end up getting what I want but the interaction with Caroline leaves me feeling used, and I don't feel inclined to use her hotel chain for any of my future business.

Sales Mistake Report Form

The Offender/Perpetrator – Enter the name of the company.

> *XYZ Hotel, salesperson Caroline.*

Sales Mistake Committed – Identify the mistake made.

> *Acting like a traditional salesperson.*

Your Statement – Clearly state the facts of what happened.

> - *The salesperson used a traditional, dated sales tactic.*
> - *She rushed the sale and tried to get the client to buy what wasn't asked for.*

Evidence – Indicate what you wanted to buy but didn't.

> *Room for 6 nights (which I did, eventually, buy).*

Future Potential Business – Outline what future business you represented.

> *Me directly: I would represent a total of 6 nights this year but also 6 nights minimum each successive year.*
> *My colleagues would represent even more business.*

Caroline's words, "The king will be $289 and the two queens will be $279. Which do you want, the king or the two queens?" were a combination of the various forms of the sales mistake of acting like a traditional salesperson. She used an old-fashioned closing technique (the alternative close), rushed the sale, and tried to sell me something I didn't ask for (which was more expensive).

This sales mistake in all its various forms is a major trust-breaker. It's one of the reasons sales has a bad reputation. Most people think of these traditional sales techniques when they think of sales, and many people feel this little knot in their stomachs when salespeople ask if they would like some help. Clients feel a sense of pressure and anticipate they are about to be manipulated.

It's not a great feeling, but this is how this sales mistake makes clients feel manipulated. Clients feel the interaction is for the benefit of the salesperson and the company, and they are the victims who are subjected to pitches and closes. No wonder clients get knots in their stomachs.

Caroline is probably not to blame. She probably had attended a recent program endorsed by her boss and her boss's boss, and she was probably doing what she was trained to do.

This is where you, the sales leader, come in. Make the decision to take 100 percent responsibility for ending the use of traditional sales techniques by your team. Your decision will help your team sell more, improve your company's reputation, and reduce clients' stomach problems. Seriously, your decision to end the use of manipulative sales techniques will improve your team's chances to create healthy and profitable long-term relationships with clients.

It's kind of ironic, isn't it? Your team members stop using traditional sales techniques, and their sales go up. To some, it may feel counterintuitive, but it works.

I remember being in a meeting with one of the top banks in the world when they shared that one of their divisions (where they had taught the team to use traditional sales techniques) had had their sales go down dramatically. They couldn't figure out why. In passing (since it wasn't part of our meeting agenda), we suggested they have the team stop selling and ask them to treat clients like they were their best friend's mother.

Well, when we met next with the leaders at that bank, the same folks were sold on not using traditional sales techniques. Sales went up by 10 percent simply by telling their team members not to sell and to get them helping clients and connecting on a personal level. I'm not saying your solution is that simple, but it may be.

Traditional sales techniques do get in the way of developing trusting relationships with clients, and you and I know trusting relationships are the foundation of repeat and referral business.

So, where are you on making the decision to take 100 percent responsibility for ending the use of traditional sales techniques?

Here's the Problem

If your team members go for the close too soon, they'll be rushing clients and they'll lose sales.

If your team members use traditional closing techniques, they'll be putting knots in their clients' stomachs, and they'll have some backtracking to do—and they'll delay or lose their sales.

If your team members deliver traditional pitches, they'll be giving monologues and missing what's important to clients. They'll miss opportunities to sell more.

In very basic terms: Traditional sales techniques make clients feel manipulated. I'm sure it's not the way you would want to feel when you buy, and it's probably not the way your clients want to feel either.

The Forensic Evidence

The following forensic evidence includes some of the clues left behind when Sales Mistake #9, Acting Like a Traditional Salesperson, is committed. Use the forensic evidence as a guideline to help you in your sales mistake detection, prevention, and rehabilitation.

Sales Numbers and Statistics – The potential statistical evidence you would notice about the perpetrators and their results.

- *Above-average percentage of short-term versus long-term clients.*
- *Prospects low in number.*
- *Fewer clients than non-perpetrating team members.*

Observable Prospect/Client Behavior – The potential evidence of the perpetrator's prospects/clients.

- *Avoid your perpetrating team member.*
- *Often end relationship with company.*

Observable Team Member Behavior – The potential evidence the perpetrator exhibits in general.

- *Has difficulty prospecting.*
- *Often will do most of the talking.*
- *Finds it hard to get business.*
- *Has a hard time filling the pipeline.*
- *Has a sales philosophy that reflects acting on clients rather than helping them.*
- *Treats sales as a numbers game rather than about people.*

Observable Coaching Behavior – The potential evidence the perpetrator exhibits in coaching sessions.

- *Hard to get to know his/her personality.*
- *Things feel superficial.*
- *Is focused on the close rather than the clients' needs.*
- *Has difficulty explaining details about clients' needs.*

What to Watch and Listen for in Your Sales Coaching

Put on your client hat for a moment. Think of the times when you wanted to buy. Let's say you are speaking with a salesperson, and you're in the process of deciding whether to buy or not. Now with this perspective, does any of the following sound familiar to you?

The salesperson asks you, "So, when do you want this delivered? Would you like it tomorrow? Or Monday?"

You're thinking: I haven't decided to buy yet. I'm not ready to answer any of those questions. You, of course, recognize the alternative close, and you're also thinking, never trust a salesperson who asks more than one question at a time. Never trust a salesperson who doesn't give you a chance to answer the first question.

"It will feel great to show it to all your colleagues."

You're thinking: *Help!!!!!!!* And you haven't even decided to buy yet. And he's already going for the close. Ever been in this position?

Or, how about the salesperson who doesn't take no for an answer? He becomes your personal sales leech. His strategy is to make you feel that the only way to get him to go away is to buy. He believes if he hounds you enough, he'll hound you into sales submission.

Or, what about the salesperson who suddenly has a new, more bubbly personality. She's smiling in a way that almost seems as if she is channeling a different person. Then, you recognize what is about to happen, and she goes into her pitch spiel. There's no stopping her.

If any of these sound familiar to you, you can be sure they sound familiar to clients, too. And if any of your team members' behaviors feel even slightly manipulative to clients, your team members are committing this sales mistake. They're acting like traditional salespeople.

You'll notice your perpetrating team members will usually do most of the talking, and will be engaged in two major forms of this sales mistake. Their sales language will include these two terms:

1. Going for the close in manipulative ways.

2. Giving pitches with no concern for clients.

Your goal is to get your perpetrating team members to stop engaging in manipulative traditional sales techniques. For the sake of your company's reputation and their sales results, have your team members focus instead on helping prospects and clients with their buying decisions.

The Toughest Part of Preventing This Sales Mistake

Some sales managers have a challenge when it comes to preventing this sales mistake: They have a team who has been using these kinds of manipulative sales techniques with decent results. If this is the case for your team, the toughest part of preventing this sales mistake will be the unlearning your team members will need to do.

In your mind, it may be best to position your team's reliance on manipulative traditional sales techniques as an addiction. Why do I say this? Because their traditional sales technique addiction (TST addiction) is fueled by the short-lived results they get. Like most victims of addiction, they don't see the negative long- and short-term effects of their TST addiction. They don't see the long-term negative impact on their sales, and they don't realize the short- and long-term harmful effects on their client relationships. It's usually clear to clients but not to them.

So you have work ahead of you to help your team members unlearn their traditional sales techniques. The work will not be done in one sales coaching session. It will take a series of sales coaching sessions and ongoing work to create your trust-based sales culture. (See Chapter 5 for more about creating this environment.)

1. Helping Clients with Their Buying Decisions

Salespeople frequently get in the way of the sale. I have found team members can often sell more, better, sooner, and more often when they focus on helping clients with their buying decisions, rather than going for the close.

The more your team focuses on helping clients, the more your team members will learn about clients' problems, so they can position themselves to help clients buy more. If your team members only go for the close, they are usually focused on selling one thing. Focusing instead on helping clients and solving clients' challenges often leads to more than just a single sale.

By putting the emphasis in your sales coaching not on forcing a sale on clients (the typical going-for-the-close), but rather on helping clients, you put your team in the position of developing greater goodwill, selling more, and earning more repeat and referral business.

Sounds like a win-win. And clients won't feel manipulated or get knots in their stomachs.

I'm going to add one other idea here. I'm going to guess you may just have some members of your team who feel they have to sell their soul to be a salesperson. These individuals are usually good people who hate using traditional sales techniques, but think they have to in order to sell. If you switch gears in your sales coaching and start putting the emphasis on helping clients rather than manipulating them, those team members who dislike using traditional sales techniques will do an internal happy dance. They will become your loyal fans and, as a result, your retention of these well-intentioned individuals will increase. Another win for reducing the use of manipulative traditional sales techniques.

As a sales leader, where do you start?

When you're sales coaching, stop using closing language (the language that implies sales is about acting on your clients rather than helping them). Remember those mirror neurons? They are the neurons in our brains that cause us to mimic the behaviors of those around us. If you stop using closing language, your team members will stop using it, too. If you start using client-helping language, they'll follow your lead. A *simple and easy first step*.

Language usually precedes behavior. So if your team members start using client-helping language, they are less likely to engage in manipulative behaviors with clients.

The next step is to focus your sales coaching on engaging your team members in sales behaviors that help clients. Ask them questions to discover what they are asking to find out what's important to their clients. Ask your team members what they heard clients say, and ask about the specifics of what clients actually said. Ask your team members what they *said* to demonstrate they understood their clients' needs. Ask your team members what they *did* to help clients with their decision making. Ask your team members what they *asked* to clarify where clients are in their decision making.

As you can see, you want to ask your team members questions so they see their sales interactions from clients' perspectives. In your sales coaching, you want to turn the tables from a focus on what they are *doing* to the client to how they are *helping* the client. This way they will not fall into the old habits of traditional sales techniques, but rather be focused on what they can do to help clients with their buying decisions.

2. Having Profitable Conversations

You've seen it, yes? The *pitch personality possession* that happens when salespeople switch into their *pitch personalities*.

Many clients are sensitive to these fake personalities salespeople adopt to give pitches, and some clients are strongly averse to them.

It's as if a different person comes into the sales conversation to deliver a canned speech. The *pitch personality* can include:

- An overly positive demeanor.
- A nauseatingly positive tone.
- A tiring intensity of energy.
- A sickeningly upbeat grin.

It feels fake and staged. Whatever personality changes that come with it are not normal and it doesn't feel genuine from the client perspective. For many clients, it's the signal the pitch is about to begin.

When salespeople are possessed by their pitch personalities, they go into a monologue about their product, droning on about things that have little or no value to clients. Typically clients wait patiently for salespeople to finish their canned speeches, ignore the tangent, and go on to ask their questions.

If salespeople stopped giving one-sided pitches, clients would breathe a sigh of relief.

Instead, salespeople could focus on having conversations that are profitable—not monologues, canned speeches, or pitches, but interactive conversations that are more profitable for both clients and salespeople.

How do you do this? Encourage your team members to be themselves and show their natural personalities. They'll discover this mutually profitable conversation that follows is more enjoyable, less time consuming, and produces more sales.

Help your team members sell more, better, sooner, and more often by getting them to stop giving meaningless pitches and instead to start focusing on interactive profitable conversations. Begin by taking the word *pitch* out of your sales coaching vocabulary. As mentioned earlier, if you stop using it, your team members will reduce their use of the word and the behavior that goes along with it.

In your sales coaching, help your team members find more conversational ways of dealing with the part of their sales conversations where they would normally have gone into a pitch. Ask them questions to help them have deeper conversations with clients, to get them thinking more about what the client wants to hear, and to challenge what they thought their clients said versus what their clients actually said. Ask them questions that will help them ask better questions of their clients, to check that what they are saying is of value to clients. Coach them to understand that clients want a dialogue, not a monologue.

Also in your sales coaching, get your team members to reflect on their conversations when a prospect decides to buy. Ask them to tell you what they did that helped the client with their buying decision. This will help them become more aware of what they can do to deemphasize the importance of traditional sales techniques.

You'll know you've done this well when your team members shift their focus from pitching clients to working with clients to find the best solutions. The word *pitch* will fade from their vocabulary and they'll focus on having more mutually profitable conversations.

For more about what your team members can say, see Chapters 2 and 3.

Try This on for Size

As you know, acting like a traditional salesperson is one of the fastest ways to break down trust. So to counteract this sales mistake and tip the scales in the other direction, get your team focused on building trust.

As mentioned earlier, you can start having your team members focus on trust by creating a trust-based sales culture. (See Chapter 5 for more details.)

There's another way you can help your team develop greater trust with clients. Your team members can do this by designing their own trust-building strategies. You can help them develop a custom strategy in your coaching sessions and in sales meetings.

The idea is for them to look at their sales conversations, processes, and activities as each having the ability to build or break down trust. Help your team members perceive everything they do and say as an opportunity to develop greater trust with clients. This kind of focus will go a long way to counteract the negative effects of their acting like traditional salespeople.

For example, get your team members to look at what they can do to build greater trust at the various times related to their sales conversations. They may identify what they can do before, during, and after their sales conversations. They may look at how they determine what trust building looks like to each client.

Another way of looking at their trust-building strategies is to look at where in your industry there are trust breakers and what your team can do to position themselves positively in contrast to these weaknesses.

By having your team members develop trust-building strategies, you help them be more focused on clients. A client-focused sales process makes it virtually impossible for your team members to act like traditional salespeople.

What This Means to Your Sales Coaching

Your sales coaching questions are the lubricant that put you in the position to listen to what is going on for your team members. Help them shift their more traditional sales approaches into more client-focused ones. Ask them questions to increase their ability to see things from the client perspective.

Here are some sample sales coaching questions you could use to deal with the sales mistake of acting like a traditional salesperson.

Sales Coaching Questions for Sales Mistake #9

"So tell me about what you asked to help your clients with this buying decision?"

"What were they interested in?"

"How do you know?"

"What did they say that gave you the impression that they were interested in that specific product?"

"What was the problem they were looking to solve?"

"What did you ask to find out about the problem they were trying to solve?"

"What was the underlying problem?"

"What did you ask to discover what the underlying problem was?"

"What was most important in the decision-making criteria?"

"What did you ask to find out what was most important to them?"

"Did you get a chance to check that what you understood matched what was said?"

"Great. What did you ask to discover this?"

"What did you ask to find out where they were in the decision-making process?"

"What did you ask to clarify if they were leaning more or less in favor of buying?"

"What did you ask to find out what was holding them back from buying?"

"Did they decide to buy?"

"Congratulations. What did you do that helped them make the decision to buy?"

"What do you think it was that made them go from feeling unsure about buying to making the decision to buy?"

"What could you have done to make the buying decision easier?"

"What could you have done to make the buying decision take less time?"

"Knowing that trust can fluctuate, when in the conversation would you say trust was at its highest between you and the clients?"

"What trust-building strategies were involved in your interactions?"

"Did trust play a factor in the decision to buy?"

"What could you have done to build more trust in the relationship?"

"Is there anything you could do now, after the fact, to build greater trust with these clients?"

"Do you have plans to ask for a referral?"

"What could you do now to increase the chances you'll get a referral?"

"Of all the ideas we've discussed, which one will you act on?"

"I like it. How about we follow up after you get that done?"

"How about you pop me off an e-mail/text when you get that done and we'll chat to see what kind of results you got? Depending on how things go, maybe we can tweak things a bit for the next time."

Pitching and Closing Preparation

To prevent this sales mistake, have your team members prepare alternatives to their traditional sales pitches and closes so they use more natural and helpful versions of what they could say. Use the following exercise to prevent this sales mistake so your team members become more client focused. You can receive a printable version of it at www.CoachingandSalesInstitute.com.

For each product, fill out this chart.

Product _____

Column 1	Column 2	Column 3	Column 4
Write out the pitches you usually use when selling this product.	Write out alternative ways you could say what you wrote in Column 1 but as an advantage to the client. (Note: The emphasis is on helping the client.)	Write out the closes you usually use when selling this product.	Write out alternative ways you could say what you wrote in Column 3 but as an advantage to the client. (Note: The emphasis is on helping the client.)

This chart will help your team plan and shift to a client focus in their selling rather than twisting the client's arm. They'll be more focused on helping clients with their buying decisions and having more profitable conversations.

To help your team prevent this Sales Mistake #9, Acting Like a Traditional Salesperson, take 100 percent responsibility to put an end to the manipulative traditional sales techniques your perpetrating team members are using (e.g., *going for the close* and *giving pitches*). Help them develop a more helpful approach by focusing on their prospects and clients. Get them to have more profitable conversations that provide greater value for prospects and clients. This kind of focus will rehabilitate your team and prevent this sales mistake from ever being experienced by prospects or clients.

Action Items from This Chapter

1. Watch and listen for team members who are using traditional sales techniques.
2. Be on the alert for clients who are feeling manipulated.
3. Assist your team members who are TST addicts (those who have the traditional sales technique addiction).

4. Take 100 percent responsibility for ending the manipulative use of traditional sales techniques.

5. Coach your team to have more mutually profitable sales conversations.

6. Stop using closing language with your team.

7. Ask your team members questions to help them shift their meaningless pitches to interactive, profitable conversations.

8. Prevent your team members from doing the pitch personality possession.

9. Eliminate pitching language with your team.

10. Help your team members develop their trust-building strategies.

CHAPTER 11

Sales Mistake #10

Treating Clients as Enemies

Picture this: You're the sales manager in a technology company, and you've been trying to reach a new target audience that has been hard to connect with—until now.

A designated leader in the industry (the national association president) approaches you to demo your product to the chapter members in her yearlong tour across the country. As a bonus, you find out she happens to be a decent salesperson. You get all that exposure (hundreds in your new target audience) at no cost to you. All you have to do is loan her the technology for the presentations. You assign Karla, one of your team members, to the project.

Karla makes a few blunders.

During her first conversation with the association president, Karla is gnarly, but the association president assumes she is having a bad day, and gives her the benefit of the doubt. She provides Karla with her presentation schedule and waits for the demo technology. Karla sends it later than promised; in fact, she sends it to the association president two weeks too late for her first two presentations.

When the association president actually receives your technology, it is faulty because Karla didn't check to make sure it was working before she sent it. To make matters worse, when the president calls to explain the problem, Karla blames the problem on her for not being tech-savvy, rather than checking out the problem.

Finally, Karla replaces the faulty technology with working technology, but by then, the president has given two additional presentations without the technology. (That makes a total of four missed opportunities to showcase your product in front of your new target audience.) *Not good.*

The association president is a positive type and chalks up Karla's challenges to Murphy's Law.

As the president travels to more chapters across the country, she uses your technology in her presentations to the members, makes sure to thank your company publicly, ensures those who are interested get your marketing materials, and displays your company's logo in all her presentations. She takes good care of your technology, and things are now going better than you could have hoped—or so you thought.

Karla hasn't contacted the association president for months. Nothing. No e-mails. No phone calls. No phone messages. Zip. Zero. Nada.

Then one day, the association president opens the following e-mail from Karla (at this point, the president is halfway through her countrywide presentation tour to the association's membership):

I am writing to follow up with you regarding the technology we have sent to you. We have made a number of attempts to contact you to evaluate this project, however, you have not been available.

Kindly make arrangements to return our technology to our offices. Please note that if the technology is not returned within seven (7) business days, this technology will be deemed to be purchased, and you will be invoiced in full—$7,366.00.

I would be happy to arrange our courier to pick up at your location tomorrow. Call or write to indicate that the package is ready for pick up.

Quite shocked, the association president forgoes the idea of demoing your technology in her remaining presentations. She doesn't want to deal with Karla anymore, and her goodwill has evaporated. The president packs up your technology and arranges for it to be ready for pick up the next day.

Neither you nor Karla knows it, but the association president was planning to buy your product. But she decides not to, based on the way she has been treated.

As the sales manager at this technology company, how would you feel about the way Karla treated the association president?

Karla was given an ideal situation in which to increase the sales of her company's product, but instead she committed the sales mistake of treating clients as enemies.

Sales Mistake Report Form

The Offender/Perpetrator – Enter the name of the company.

> *XYZ Technology Company, salesperson Karla.*

Sales Mistake Committed – Identify the mistake made.

> *Treating clients as enemies.*

Your Statement – Clearly state the facts of what happened.

> - *The salesperson blamed the potential client for product errors.*
> - *The salesperson treated potential client as an enemy. After all, the potential client was helping to sell the product.*
> - *The salesperson threatened the potential client.*
> - *The salesperson implied the potential client was not responding to communication, blaming her for the salesperson's lack of follow-up.*

Evidence – Indicate what you wanted to buy but didn't.

> *The technology.*

Future Potential Business – Outline what future business you represented.

> - *The association president directly would represent one or two sets of the technology.*
> - *Her professional peers would represent hundreds of potential clients.*

In defense of Karla, as the association president originally felt, she might have been going through a tough phase in her life, but the reality is: She had the ability to influence the sale of her product to hundreds, and tainted the opportunity.

While we can try to explain her behavior, Karla was having a bad day. (*For several months?*) Karla has a gruff personality. (*Then should she be in a client-facing position?*)

Karla was new to the job. (*Then who's responsible for her training?*) No matter how much explaining one can do, there is no excuse for treating clients as enemies.

You may be blessed with a team that doesn't commit this mistake. You may be thinking, "Thank goodness, my team never does anything like this." Yet, how do you know?

The association president in this example chose not to provide feedback to the sales manager. So he doesn't know and probably never will. Maybe your team's prospects are choosing not to provide you with feedback either. Disconcerting, isn't it? This sales mistake could be happening on your team and you may not even know it.

Here's the Problem

If your team members change agreements with clients, they'll remove all the goodwill they created and lose sales (as Karla did with the association president).

If your team members raise their voices with clients, they'll turn clients off and lose sales.

If your team members set clients up and blame them for their poor follow-through, they'll ruin their opportunities to create goodwill and they will lose sales.

If your team members are treating clients as enemies, they'll lose sales and negatively affect your company's reputation.

It bears repeating. If your team members are committing this sales mistake, they're losing sales and potentially creating a negative reputation for your product(s) and your company.

The Forensic Evidence

The following forensic evidence includes some of the clues left behind when Sales Mistake #10, Treating Clients as Enemies, is committed. Use the forensic evidence as a guideline to help you in your sales mistake detection, prevention, and rehabilitation.

Sales Numbers and Statistics – The potential statistical evidence you would notice about the perpetrators and their results.

- *Negative effect on long-term sales.*
- *Referrals stop abruptly.*
- *Potential repeat business ends for no apparent reason.*
- *Negative comments in social media.*

Observable Prospect/Client Behavior – The potential evidence of the perpetrator's prospects and clients.

- *Has no loyalty to perpetrating team member.*
- *Will stop buying without giving feedback as to why.*
- *Often complains online.*
- *Non-responsive to further inquiries.*

Observable Team Member Behavior – The potential evidence the perpetrator exhibits in general.

- *Jumps the gun.*
- *Often perceives negative before positive.*
- *Sees things from one perspective and has trouble viewing things from others' perspectives.*

Observable Coaching Behavior – The potential evidence the perpetrator exhibits in coaching sessions.

- *Often blames clients.*
- *Builds negative cases about clients.*
- *Doesn't take any ownership of problems.*

What to Watch and Listen for in Your Sales Coaching

The whole point of sales is to attract and retain clients. When your team members commit this mistake, their actions fly in the face of this fundamental purpose of sales.

If you know you have team members who are committing this mistake, you'll probably feel those team members are working against you and their sales targets. Most sales managers' level of frustration with these perpetrating team members is high. This poses a challenge to your sales coaching. It can make you less effective than you normally are.

The same frustration you feel when dealing with your perpetrating team members is similar to the frustration they feel toward their enemy clients. It's this frustration that causes your perpetrating team members to treat clients as enemies.

Your team members' reasons for treating clients as enemies can be because:

- They don't care.
- They didn't understand what happened.
- They didn't realize how important things are to the client.
- They did what they saw other team members do in a similar situation.
- They didn't make the connection how their behavior could be interpreted.

Whatever your perpetrating team members' reasons for treating clients as enemies, with your sales coaching, you can help turn things around and prevent this sales mistake from happening.

You'll notice your perpetrating team members are not naturally inclined to think from the clients' perspective. They'll do unusual (and sometimes unthinkable) things to prospects and clients. Think of Karla and what she did to the association president. You may sometimes think your perpetrating team members are not working on your sales team but on the competition's.

Some of the behaviors your perpetrating team members may be engaging in include:

- Changing agreements with clients without letting them know.
- Delivering something different than promised.
- Using an angry tone with clients.
- Blaming clients (so your perpetrating team members look better).

Your perpetrating team members will most likely demonstrate a low ability to consider clients' perspectives in their actions.

A Lesson from James

We're in an all-you-can-eat sushi restaurant. For the first time ever, my husband chooses to order the sushi himself. Though he had eaten sushi regularly, he had never ordered it. He very proudly takes the order form and bends it in such a way that I can't see what he is writing. He proceeds to fill out the order. He wants to surprise me with my favorites.

The waitress takes the order from him.

My husband turns to me saying, "I ordered some appetizers and then we can choose what we want afterwards." We go on with our conversation.

Our appetizers start to arrive. The first plate has 36 pieces on it. The second plate of appetizers has 24 pieces. To give you some perspective, I usually eat 12 pieces for a meal. And there are still more appetizers to come.

My husband, looking rather panicky, ran from the table to our waitress saying, "Don't bring us anymore." As you know, the all-you-can-eat sushi restaurant rules are: What you don't eat, you buy at regular price.

A minute later our waitress comes to our table with two more plates. Sushi and sashimi.

My husband is beside himself with embarrassment. We now have more than 90 pieces of sushi, enough for at least 7 people. He realizes that when he filled out the order form, he had mistaken *one roll* of sushi (6–8 pieces) to mean *one piece* of sushi.

We can see our waitress speaking in hushed tones to a tall man behind the sushi counter. My husband is turning white (he hates to spend money on food). The tall man makes a direct line for our table. My husband starts to slump down in his seat.

The tall man, James, looms over our table and introduces himself saying, "No worries." Turning to my husband, he explains the rules of the restaurant, "Normally we would charge you for the food you haven't eaten but since this is your first time ordering, we'll pack up the extra for you as takeout . . . no charge."

Color starts coming back to my husband's face.

Impressed with how James turned a difficult situation into an opportunity, I say, "James, you handled that so well. You could have charged us for each piece we didn't eat and sent us on our way. But instead, you are eating the cost of our mistake."

James responds without taking a breath, "If I treat you like friends, you'll be back. If I charge you, I won't see you again. I want to see you again because you are my friends. I wouldn't charge a friend. So I won't charge you." And with a smile, he adds, ". . . this time."

Then he stretches out his arms to the busy restaurant saying, "They're all my friends."

(To give you some context, the restaurant next door, that serves great food, is empty.)

Needless to say, my husband and I are loyal customers of James' restaurant and recommend the restaurant to all our friends.

The moral of the story: You want your team treating clients like friends, not enemies. When clients are treated like friends, they engage in repeat business and give referrals. If you have perpetrating team members who treat clients as enemies, they're losing opportunities for future business.

1. Treat Clients Like Friends

It may seem obvious to you to treat clients like friends, but to your perpetrating team members, it's not so obvious. For some reason, they don't see it. What is crystal clear to you looks muddy to them. If they saw things the way you did, they wouldn't treat clients as enemies. And just like you think your perspective on this topic is better or more accurate than theirs, they think the same way about what happened with the client they treated like an enemy.

I'm sure Karla justified her treatment of the association president to her sales manager. She probably painted a negative picture of the president to distract from her sales mistake of treating the customer like an enemy.

Most likely your perpetrating team members will try to bring you over to their negative perception of the client, just like you want them to see the situation through your friendly lens.

To effectively coach team members who commit this sales mistake, it's helpful to understand the dynamic. It will help you be more effective in your coaching.

Your perpetrating team members' attempts to bring you over to their side are the driving force of their desire to share what happened. With this in mind, let them describe all the intricate details of how they are victims at the hands of terrible clients, enemies of your company. Listen to understand their perspectives. You don't have to agree with them; you just need to understand them.

Understanding your team members' perspective will cause two things to happen: One, your team members will feel heard, which will probably be their driving force at this point in your conversation. Two, you will know what to ask to help them shift their perception of the particular clients.

Once they have replayed their version of their client conversations, ask them questions to replay their conversations from the clients' perspective. This is where your ability to recall what they said will be immensely helpful.

This part of your sales coaching session is not meant to be about putting your team members in their place, but rather a curious exploration of what things might have looked and sounded like from the clients' perspective. In most cases, well-intentioned perpetrators will have eureka moments and will suddenly see things from the clients' perspective.

If your sales coaching conversation is going well, you can also ask questions about other people's perspectives. For example, you may ask how other observers, like the clients' peers or bosses, might interpret the clients' behavior.

Including other perspectives in your sales coaching questions can help your team members see things more objectively. Yet, as mentioned above, only include other perspectives if the sales coaching is going well and your team members are opening up. If your team members' egos are involved, they can become more defensive. The quality of your sales coaching conversation will determine if you include additional perspectives.

Two Ways to Discover If This Sales Mistake Exists

To make your coaching job easier, you may be happy to know there are two simple ways to discover if your team members are committing this sales mistake. One comes from considering the behaviors of your team members' prospects. The second comes from evaluating the observable behaviors of your team members.

When coaching your team members, don't coach them only on the prospects who have become clients, but also on the prospects they haven't heard from recently. Individuals who have been treated as enemies often stop interacting with or responding to your team members.

With this in mind, include a review of prospects who seem to have dropped off your team members' radars. Coach your team members on the details of their last interaction with each specific prospect. By adding this to your sales coaching, you ensure you catch the prospects who might have been treated as enemies by your team members. You can then coach your team members on how to earn back goodwill with these prospects.

You'll find it helpful to notice the observable behaviors of your team members, such as voice quality and body language, when they talk about clients. These can be your clues to ask further questions to discover if your team members are committing this sales mistake. In your sales coaching, comment on what you noticed about their voice quality and body language that demonstrates they are frustrated with clients. You may say something like, "I noticed your voice just got louder as you talked about that client. What's that about?"

This kind of noticing in your sales coaching will get your team members opening up and sharing details of their perspectives of what happened with their clients. This open discussion will help you determine if your team members did actually treat clients as enemies.

2. Customize All Follow-Up Communications

If your company is like most, you have sales processes you follow. For example, there may be form letters or e-mails that go out. There may be a process in place to pass dead accounts on to new salespeople on the team.

At Karla's company, they pass dead accounts on to the new guy. The same day the technology was picked up from the association president's office, she received an e-mail from the new guy, and for context, the president was still feeling the sting of Karla's sales mistake.

The e-mail from the new guy was a standard sales letter extolling the virtues of his company's technology for someone who had never seen or used it. As you know, the president was well aware of the virtues of the technology because she used it in some of her presentations to her association members. I've removed any identifying information from the body of the e-mail, but this is how it ended.

> At your convenience, I would like to book a free 30-minute demonstration, either onsite or via web, showcasing the features and benefits of such a powerful business tool.
>
> Thank you for your time, I look forward to hearing from you soon.

Nowhere in the e-mail did the new guy acknowledge or hint he knew anything about what the association president had done for the company. *Ouch.*

Nowhere in the e-mail did he make note of the fact she had used the technology already. *Ouch.*

And nowhere in the e-mail did he thank her for exposing the association members (their target audience) to their product. *Ouch.*

The new guy demonstrated no knowledge of what happened previously. He was focused on selling the product and not on the association president. I wonder if the new guy had customized his e-mail (treating the president as a friend), might he have saved the sale?

As an FYI, the association president continued to get a series of these types of e-mails from the new guy. Each one is a form e-mail with no customization, focused strictly on selling the product. If you were the association president, what would be your perception of these e-mails? Would they increase or decrease your goodwill towards the company?

After your perpetrating team members treat clients as enemies, it's important to keep an eagle eye on subequent communications that go out to that client. You don't want clients irritated further.

Encourage your team members to be vigilant after they have treated clients as enemies. You may need to go so far as to help them tweak template e-mails or letters your company typically uses. You and your team can't afford to be sending out the typical communications to clients who have been treated as enemies.

What This Means to Your Sales Coaching

As you know, your sales coaching questions put you in the position to listen to what is going on for your team members as well as what is working and not working for them.

Here are some sample sales coaching questions you could use to prevent the sales mistake of treating clients as enemies.

Sales Coaching Questions for Sales Mistake #10

"Let's look at your interactions with your prospects who have not been responding to your follow-up. Who do you want to start with first?"

"Tell me, what are the different interactions you had with her?"

"What does that work out to be, two interactions?"

"Let's look at each one individually, just as an overview, and see what we discover. How about you start with the first interaction?"

"On a scale of 1 to 10, how do you think it went (1 being it went poorly, and 10 being it went really well)?"

"How about the next interaction? Tell me about that." *(As your team member tells you about this one, you notice she seems frustrated.)*

"I noticed your voice went up and your body tightened as you talked. What is that about?" *(Let's say your team member goes on about how frustrated she was with the client and, in the process, gives you the sense there may be an interesting client perspective on what she did.)*

"Tell me what you said to the client."

"How did the client respond?"

"Where was your level of frustration at this point?"

"Where do you think your client's level of frustration was?"

"If you were the client, where would yours be?"

"If you were the client, what would you be thinking at this point in the conversation?"

"So what happened next in that conversation?" *(Let's say your team member goes on about how she made sure the client understood her perspective.)*

"What was it that you wanted her to understand?"

"How did she respond to what you said?"

"What was it that she was wanting you to understand?"

"What did you do to demonstrate you understood what she wanted you to know?"
   (Let's say your team member said she did nothing to demonstrate she understood.)

"What could you have done to demonstrate you understood?"

"If you were the client, what would you have wanted to hear or see to be reassured that you were understood?"

"So what happened next in the conversation?"

"If you were the client, would you have been more or less inclined to buy?"
   (Let's say your team member says less.)

"What could you have done to increase the likelihood she would be more inclined to buy?"

"So, based on our conversation, what would you do differently if you were in a similar situation again?"

"What one nugget can you use in the next week?"

"Sounds like a plan! When can we touch base with each other at the end of the next week to see how things are going?"

"Before we say goodbye, what might you do about the client we were talking about? Is there any follow-up you can do to regain some goodwill?"

"When will you get a chance to do that?"

"How about we add that to our agenda next week to see how that goes too?"

Client-Friendly Preparation

You can help your team treat prospects more appropriately by providing your team members with opportunities to prepare to treat prospects as friends. Use the following exercise to prevent your team from committing this sales mistake. You can receive a printable version of it at www.CoachingandSalesInstitute.com.

Have your team members fill out this chart based on their sales activities for the past week, couple of weeks, or month.

Column 1	Column 2	Column 3	Column 4	Column 5
List the prospects who have not responded to your messages this week/ month.	What happened in your last interaction with the prospect listed in Column 1 that caused them to lose interest?	What could be the prospect's perspective of what happened (what you wrote in Column 2)?	Brainstorm what you can do to earn some goodwill from the prospect listed in Column 1.	What would be the most effective thing to do for this prospect from your list in Column 4?

This chart will help your team members become more conscious of how to treat their prospects better. It will increase their awareness of their prospects' perspectives so they can better plan how to develop or earn back goodwill.

As you help your team members to prevent the Sales Mistake #10, Treating Clients as Enemies, focus first on hearing your team members' perspectives, and then on opening their minds to the clients' perspective. By listening to your team members, you demonstrate for them what it's like to have someone hear their perspective. They'll then understand the value of demonstrating to their clients that they hear the other side of things. This openness to clients' perspectives is the key to rehabilitating your perpetrating team members.

Action Items from This Chapter

1. Be on the lookout for perpetrating team members' behaviors.

2. Determine with your team which prospects have not responded to your team members.

3. Review their last interactions with those prospects.

4. Listen to your team members share their perception of enemy clients.

5. Engage in curious exploration of what happened.

6. Notice when your team members seem frustrated with clients.

7. Coach your team members to understand their clients' perspectives.

8. Brainstorm what your team members can do to earn goodwill.

9. Set a standard of customizing all follow-up communications.

10. Get your team members to treat clients like friends.

CHAPTER

12

Making Your Sales Coaching Sustainable

Imagine you're a great singer. In fact, you're so good you are one of the four Canadian Tenors. You get the call of a lifetime. You've just been asked to perform on *The Oprah Show*. You pinch yourself. You're nervous but excited.

The day comes. You walk out on stage with your fellow Canadian Tenors, and everything seems to move in slow motion. You finally get to hug Oprah and sit down beside her.

Oprah starts the interview. You chat about working together, how you all met and chose your songs. You each take turns answering Oprah's questions, except one question which you answer together. The question is, "Who's your singing hero?" You all answer, "Celine Dion."

The details of the rest of your conversation are hazy. You're so excited to be on Oprah's show. Yet you're nervous because you still have to sing.

Oprah cuts to break. You and the other three Canadian Tenors get ready to sing when you come back from the commercial break. It's time. You and your three melodious buddies start singing. It's going great. The audience loves it. Oprah loves it. You're all in the flow. You're singing well. This is one of the highlights of your singing career. Life can't get better than this.

Then, the crowd roars even louder.

You notice some of the audience members seem to be looking through you. You turn your head slightly and catch of glimpse of someone behind you. Your buddies haven't noticed yet. *It's Celine Dion!*

You can't stop singing to tell your buddies or you'll ruin the song. And you can't nudge them either because it will break their singing. So you continue singing, and finally, one by one, your buddies notice.

Then Celine joins in and sings with you. You're singing with *Celine Dion! And you thought life couldn't get better!*

Then something happens that you can't explain. You and your fellow tenors are singing better than you were even moments ago. Somehow you are all singing better than you ever have before.

As you notice the improvement in all your singing, your eyes water. You wonder if your buddies have noticed. You look at them and their eyes are watering too. You all exchange a knowing look.

This is the height of your singing career.

You have no words to describe what you just experienced but you'll never forget the feeling, and you decide to affectionately call it the Celine Effect.

Welcome back to the world of reality.

It's this Celine Effect that will happen for your team members when you commit to sales coaching them regularly and effectively. With this focus, they'll perform better and surpass their sales targets. When you coach your team well, you make your sales coaching really stick for significant sales improvement.

You're now armed with the sales coaching insights from this book to prevent sales mistakes, so your team members can have more profitable sales conversations. The question is: What are *you* going to do now?

Give yourself time to practice what you have learned about sales coaching from this book. It's in the execution of these sales coaching ideas where the magic will happen.

Keep the powerful effect of struggle in mind when you sales coach. Don't be the supplier of all the answers. Let your team members struggle through their thinking. Remember the butterfly story from Chapter 1? As counterintuitive as it may seem, letting your team members struggle so they develop their thinking is the key to improving their performance, and giving you back some valuable time. The by-product will be a better client experience.

How do you do this? By focusing on what *you* do during your sales coaching sessions:

- Demonstrate your listening.
- Ask questions.
- Provide relevant information.

Of these three, the most important focus is asking questions. You want to be asking strong sales coaching questions to get your team members talking and thinking—and to get yourself listening. Your questions will put you in the position of really knowing what is going on so you can be more helpful.

Knowing what sales coaching questions to ask is both an art and a science. It's an art because you have to constantly adapt to what is happening in the moment during your sales coaching sessions. What works in one conversation won't necessarily work in the next because each team member is different. Each of them thinks differently, processes information differently, and sells differently. On top of that, they're dealing with different clients with specific needs, so tailoring your questions is key to your sales coaching.

Despite this, there are commonalities to your questions and strategy that are driven by the science of sales coaching. There are aspects to your sales coaching questions that consistently give you and your team members the results you want. By asking effective questions, you'll make your sales coaching stick, and create better, sustainable results.

Sales Coaching Question Guidelines

In this book, you've been given sales coaching questions to assist you. To ensure your questions are effective, you probably would appreciate some guidelines .

1. Don't Do Theory

Stick to specifics when you ask your questions. Why? Most salespeople know what they should do, but they don't always do it.

It's like asking people what they should eat for a healthy lifestyle. They know the right things to eat, but if you ask them what they ate for a specific meal, you'll often discover they didn't follow their own advice. Instead of eating a green salad with grilled chicken breast, they ate fried chicken, fries, and a double chocolate brownie banana split.

The same holds true for your team members' sales interactions. If you ask them what *should* happen at the beginning of a sales interaction, they'll give the right answer: Sales conversations should begin with discovery questions. Yet, if you ask them to share specifics from one of their recent sales conversations, you'll find that instead of asking some good questions to identify the client's needs, they started by telling the client about the history of the company (without checking if the client was interested). *Ouch.*

If you choose to coach what they could have done (the theory), your sales coaching conversations will stay at the abstract theoretical level, and result in little to no improvement in their sales behaviors.

If instead you coach the concrete specifics of what happened, your sales coaching conversations will be focused on how salespeople can do better next time, resulting in improved sales behaviors.

When you ask your team members about their specific sales interactions, get them talking about what really happens in their sales world. This way, your sales coaching conversations are grounded in reality and can more easily be applied to their daily client interactions. Coach reality, not theory, to get some serious sales improvement.

2. Ask Mostly about the Situation

Make the majority of your questions about one specific sales situation. Don't let your coaching sessions lose focus and bounce around between different sales conversations. Instead, use your questions to get deeply into one conversation.

You'll find that the insights and sales improvement that come from this specific approach will get your team performing better, sooner. You can liken it to someone doing renovations to their house for the first time. By working on one room at a time, they can leverage what they learn in each room and apply it to subsequent projects, seeing improvement in every one.

3. Don't Interrogate

Sales coaching is not an interrogation. It's a conversation designed to help your team members perform better. Your role is to be on their side, helping them, not interrogating them. Interrogation can be interpreted as having the intent of putting them in their place.

Use your sales coaching questions as an integral part of developing your relationships and demonstrating your support of your team members.

Select your words carefully. One word can make the difference between a helpful conversation and an interrogation. For example, the use of the word "why" can put some people on the defensive. No matter how warm and friendly your intonation, "why" can have a negative effect, and change the positive direction of your sales coaching conversations. I can hear you saying, "But what do I say instead?"

Instead of saying "Why?" consider using a phrase like, "How come?" And instead of saying "Why did you . . .?" you could ask "What were your reasons for . . .?" or "What was your thinking behind . . .?"

With simple changes in your language, your team members will feel as if they are working with you to increase their sales, rather than feel they are working against you in an interrogation.

4. Focus on Being Helpful

This may seem like an obvious guideline yet sometimes sales coaching conversations can go off track for various reasons (e.g., you're having a bad day, your team member just finished a call with an irate client, etc.). How do you know? Your sales coaching conversation will start to feel like a power game rather than a helpful interaction.

If you are feeling like you are not being helpful with your questions in a sales coaching conversation, take a moment, own it, and say something like, "I'm feeling like I'm not being very helpful right now. Can you give me some feedback? How helpful is this for you?" Then listen. Don't defend or explain. Just take in your team members' feedback. Thank them and either switch gears or reschedule your sales coaching session. I mention this because we are all human and we will experience good days and bad days.

5. Always Include a Commitment

Every sales coaching conversation should include your team members committing to using their new sales approach. You don't want to end your sales coaching conversations without these commitments.

These kinds of commitments from your team members are the foundation of their ongoing, incremental sales improvement. Without them, your sales coaching conversations become nothing more than just hopeful talk.

Your commitment questions can be as simple as, "Of all the ideas we discussed, which one are you going to use next time you are in a similar situation?"

These new approaches your team members commit to are not meant to be long-term commitments, but rather short-term trials to see how the new approaches affect their sales results. They are test runs whose value is measured later by their level of success.

Do you hear the sales coaching mantra? Commitment. Commitment. Commitment.

6. Follow-Up

At the end of each of your sales coaching conversations, include how and when you are going to follow up with your team members. By scheduling the follow-up with specific time frames, your team members will be more willing to try their new approaches.

Building follow-up into your sales coaching breaks your team members' new sales commitments into manageable chunks. They will be more willing to commit to new approaches for a short period of time rather than engaging in new behaviors for an indefinite period of time. Your follow-up questions facilitate your team members trying and engaging in new behaviors.

These questions may include, "When would be a good time for us to follow up with one another to see how your new approach is working for you?" or "How about we touch base next week to see how it went? What day might work for you?"

When you are sure to schedule follow-ups into your sales coaching, you convert what might have been a pleasant but easily forgotten conversation into a profitable sales improvement conversation.

7. *Explain Why*

Sales coaching is not about getting your team members to do something, but rather about working *with* them. People like to understand why they are being asked to participate in professional development activities. For this reason, provide context for your team members by explaining why you're initiating coaching sessions and what they can expect to experience.

Before you explain the *why* of coaching, ask your team members about their expectations and understanding of sales coaching. Inquire about what they think they're expected to do in their coaching sessions, and what they expect of you during the coaching. Discover the perceived level of value they feel your sales coaching can have on their sales.

This kind of inquiry, before you get into the conversation about why sales coaching, will help you discover what to say and what not to say.

You may be saying to yourself, "I don't need to explain why we are doing sales coaching to my team because we've had sales coaching here at our company for years." If this is the case in your company, the need to explain what coaching looks like is even greater. If your company is like most, the sales coaching your team has experienced is probably not sales coaching, as described in this book. Most companies do either sales-stat reviews or sales downloading. If this is the case, your team members will have some unlearning to do, which can sometimes be tougher and more time-consuming.

Whether your company has an established sales coaching program or not, your team members will need to know how you define coaching, and why they're being coached by you. You may want to include some of the following points in your explanation:

- "My role, as your sales coach, is to help you sell better."
- "Your role is to examine what happened and share your thoughts."
- "I'll ask you a lot of questions."
- "There are no wrong answers."
- "It will feel like an exploration of what happened during your sales interaction."
- "I'll do a lot of listening."
- "You'll do most of the talking."

- "We'll get into the nitty-gritty details of your sales conversations."
- "We'll also explore your thinking behind what happened."
- "We'll look at alternative sales approaches and you'll chose the one that best suits you and your prospects/clients."
- "We might look for places where additional information could be helpful."
- "You'll be actively involved in your learning process and your sales strategy."
- "You'll determine what you can do better next time you are in a similar sales situation."
- "It's about applying what you know better."
- "Our focus will be on what is most helpful for the client, and what feels most like you."
- "The goal is for you and me to be working as a team to help you sell more, better, sooner, and more often."

Notice it is not just about what *your team members* will be doing, but also about what *you* will be doing to support them. When explaining the *why* of coaching, include what both of you will be doing so they understand it is about you helping them do better. You also want them to fully understand the concept that the more they share, the more helpful you can be and the better their sales results will be.

Depending on how your team members respond, you may also discover the need to explain what coaching is not:

- Coaching is not about you telling them what to do, but helping them discover what would be the most helpful for their client.
- Coaching is not about you acting on them, but asking them questions to help them find the most effective approach for next time.
- Coaching is not about you lecturing them, but working together to find the most effective approach for when they are in a similar situation.
- Coaching is not about determining one "right" way of selling, but figuring out the most helpful way for each client.

You can increase your team members' performance by helping them better understand why they, and you, are engaged in coaching. As you know, the better they understand what to expect in their sales coaching sessions with you, the more helpful you can be to them. And the more helpful you are, the better their sales results will be.

Follow these seven sales coaching question guidelines and you'll be well on your way to becoming an awesome sales coach.

A Dose of Reality

Just like your team members have sales mistakes they commit, you have sales coaching mistakes you commit. *Sorry to break the news.*

The one sales coaching mistake I see happening over and over in corporations is that of not providing enough feedback. In almost every corporation we've worked with, the sales leaders and team members feel that they don't give, or get, as much feedback as they would like.

Here's a test. When was the last time you gave some feedback to each of your team members? When was the last time you gave every member on your team some feedback? Last quarter? Last month? A couple of weeks ago? If your goal is to help them do better today than they did yesterday, is the present frequency of your sales coaching enough?

And here's another test: When was the last time you received some feedback? I don't mean a pat on the back—I mean some valuable feedback that helped you do better.

And here's yet another test: When was the last time you asked for feedback from your team members?

Suffice it to say, most leaders don't provide enough feedback based on the perception of their team members, and most leaders don't get enough feedback from their teams.

With this in mind, build feedback into every sales coaching conversation. Make sure to not only give feedback, but to receive it as well. Provide your feedback in a coach-like fashion and it will be most effective.

Feedback is More Effective When. . .

Feedback can be most effective when it is given in the form of questions.

The reason we give feedback is to increase our receivers' awareness of what is working (or not working), so they can select a more effective approach next time. By using questions in your feedback, you help your team members receive feedback more openly, change their behaviors more quickly, and focus on improvement more consistently.

For example: Let's say a team member, Sam, comes to you for some feedback and coaching on how he did with a client today. One way you might start the conversation is with questions like:

- "On a scale of 1 to 10 (1 being very poor and 10 being outstanding), how would you rank what you did with that client?"
- If Sam was working on a specific sales skill, like asking discovery questions, you may make the last part of your question more specific like: "How would you rank the quality of the discovery questions you asked that client?"

Sam responds with a 7. You would continue with questions like the ones below:

- "What makes it a 7 versus an 8?"
- "What makes it a 7 versus a 6?"
- "What could you have done to make it a 9 or a 10?"
- "How would you like to rank next time?"
- "What are you going to do differently next time to get that ranking?"
- "When can I follow up with you to see how it went?"

In contrast, you could have not used questions in your feedback and simply stated, "Sam, based on what you described, that sales interaction was a solid 6 but to make it a 10, you should have _____." It would have taken less time in the short term, but it probably wouldn't create the lasting effect you'd like.

How much thinking would Sam have done if you simply told him what to do? How much ownership would Sam have if the ideas came from you instead of him? By asking questions when you provide feedback, you increase your team members' ability to process and integrate what they learned. This results in better sales performance in the long term.

Sales Success is Contagious

As your team's sales results improve with your coaching, you'll get the Celine Effect happening on your team. To facilitate this, consider having your team members share success stories during your sales meetings. Their sales successes will be contagious.

As they hear their teammates talking about how they surpassed their sales targets, and what they did to get those results, they'll start to see what is possible. They'll start to believe more is possible.

When your first team member breaks a sales target your team members never thought possible, it'll be like the historic day in the world of running when Roger Bannister broke the four-minute mile barrier. Before Bannister, a sub four-minute mile was a runner's dream, not a reality. Athletes and scientists alike thought that it was physically impossible for humans to run that fast, but once other runners' minds opened to the real possibility of a sub four-minute mile, the world of running shifted. Within one year, 30 other runners broke the four-minute mile. When beliefs change, results change.

I wonder what the effect will be when one of your team members breaks one of your company's sales barriers. What will be the impact on your other team members? Imagine what sales limits they'll break when they know they're capable of more.

As the coach, it all begins with you. By sales coaching your team members, you influence them to perform better on a continuous basis. The Quantum Coaching

Effect will kick in (see Chapter 1), and your team members will look forward to their coaching with you. As a result, one of your team members will break their sales targets, allowing the Celine Effect to work its magic. One team member's success will influence the others and drive them to do even better.

It is the combination of the Quantum Coaching Effect (where you affect your team members) and the Celine Effect (where your team members influence one another's performance) that is the ultimate in sales coaching. Make it your goal. Both you and your team members will appreciate it.

It all comes down to the simple concept of coaching your team members to make new neurological connections so they can think, perform, and sell better.

Action Items from This Chapter

1. Give yourself time to practice your sales coaching.
2. Focus on your quality sales coaching questions.
3. Don't do theory.
4. Ask mostly about the situation.
5. Don't interrogate your team members.
6. Focus on being helpful.
7. Include commitment in every one of your sales coaching sessions.
8. Be sure to build follow-up into your sales coaching.
9. Explain to your team members the *why* of sales coaching.
10. Provide feedback in a coach-like fashion.

Bonus Chapter

Leveraging Your CRM during Sales Coaching

"**I** LOVE our CRM!!!"

This is the response of the division's sales support person, May, when I ask about their customer relationship management system. Since I'm not sure if she is just an overly enthusiastic type when it comes to technology, I follow up with, "*Have you found it's made a difference to the team's sales?*"

"Yes, it's made a huge difference. After all, what gets measured, gets done."

May continues explaining the benefits of the system. Of course, I ask about how they decide their metrics. May responds, "Our sales VP meets with his boss and they determine the goals and objectives, and then they break that down with the help of the sales managers into the behaviors they measure."

I'm thinking: great answer, but where are the reps' perspectives taken into consideration with the setup of their system. You can predict my next question: "*Have there been any challenges getting the reps to use the system?*"

"Actually, we haven't had any challenges. The reps all fill out the system. It's mobile. They're on the road most of the time and the mobile nature of our system makes it easy for them to access it at all times. It's on the cloud."

May's answer feels somewhat utopian so I ask, "*A lot of managers complain that their salespeople don't use their CRM well. What's your secret?*" May's brief response takes her answer from utopia to sales reality. It's a major key to the success of their CRM.

"Buy-in."

"Tell me more about that. What do you do to get buy-in from the reps?"

"Well, before we implemented the system, I met with the reps. I asked them what they needed from the system to help them sell better. I asked about the fields and the notes that they needed. And I shared with them what information management needed and why, so they understood the purpose and function of each item. Getting them to understand the function and how we are going to use the data was important."

I'm thinking, *brilliant*. No wonder they're having such success with their CRM.

Successful Implementation and Usage of Your CRM

A CRM can be a vital tool to improving sales. Notice I didn't say it was the cure for your sales challenges.

When a CRM is leveraged with sales coaching, it can be a powerful catalyst to selling more. The potential of this dynamic duo is first impacted by the leaders in your organization. It's about creating a solid foundation for your CRM and your sales coaching.

Successful CRM Setup

Let's look at the components of setting up a CRM for success. Now, before you check out, thinking that this next bit of content may not apply to you, read it carefully, because within it are keys to ensure you're using your CRM to maximize your and your team's performance. I interviewed some experts from the CRM world and they'll share their secrets for setting up a CRM for success.

As you review this next section, look for the one idea you can implement within your company to improve your team's sales.

Let's be clear. A CRM alone is not your savior. As Gerhard Gschwandtner, founder and publisher of *Selling Power*, reminds us, "Technology gives you a foundation of science upon which you can construct the art of selling." He goes on to explain that the context of your CRM is what determines its success.

For example, when you're setting up a CRM, ensure it is set up in the context of your company's strategy, sales training, sales coaching (we'll get into this in greater detail), recruiting, and onboarding. These changing needs require that your CRM be agile. In essence, see your CRM as part of the technology to set your people (and your customers) up for success. You'll find this perception helpful with your overall sales coaching success and CRM usage.

Let's get into further detail. *Ready for those secrets?*

There are three basic aspects to setting up your CRM for success:

1. Company Strategy

The first step to aligning a company's strategy with its CRM (and later, its sales coaching) is to help everyone involved to better understand what a CRM can do for their organization. For example, we know technology has changed the way people buy, and has therefore transformed the roles of the salesperson and the sales manager (more on this later in the chapter). As Paul Greenberg, author of *CRM at the Speed of Light*, states, "What worked in the past doesn't work in the present."

Before aligning your CRM with your business strategy, it's helpful to better understand how Sales 2.0 has changed the nature of your business and your sales processes, how social media has helped to further define the profile of your ideal customer, and how you connect with, deepen, and grow your customer relationships.

Mark Woollen, VP Product Marketing at Salesforce.com, shares, "Many companies are experiencing success at the margins of CRM. They begin to realize they have a good reporting system but they still don't have a sales system."

Rob Saul, President of Serex Sales Automation Services, reiterates this valuable sales perspective, "Your CRM is about nurturing the relationship with the customer."

Next in the strategy conversation is clarification of what information your organization needs to make its decisions. These needs become the rough framework for the setup of your CRM, but the work doesn't stop there.

David Beard, CRM Principal at Sage, shares, "Connect CRM design and usage to business strategy. Once a goal is set, what are you going to do with your software to help your people report on it, work to it, and deliver on it?"

Then comes the heavy lifting.

2. Inter-Department Collaboration

Allow me to start by asking you how often you find you're having conversations with other departments. If you are like most sales leaders, you're not having a lot dialogue with the marketing department. If you are, you're the exception to the rule. Congratulations.

It's almost an accepted practice in many organizations for marketing to be siloed in their world and for you, in sales, to be siloed in yours. The setup of your CRM is more successful when sales and marketing (as well as other departments) work together.

As Courtney Wiley, Director of Global Digital Demand Generation at Oracle, points out, "Regardless of technology, the relationship between sales and marketing is paramount to setting up your CRM for success."

Beard explains that this philosophy is based on the way technology has changed how people buy. He suggests, "Marketing is becoming a key to the sales engine." *Hear him out.*

"Salespeople really need to educate their prospects with relevant content earlier in the selling cycle and the marketing funnel," he says.

Think about it. Because of technology, clients are more educated and more product savvy than they have ever been. For this reason, salespeople need to be ready to speak with leads who are further along in their decision making because of the information they have gleaned online or from colleagues and peers.

Beard continues, "Customers are often further down the buying cycle once they get to the point of interacting with your selling cycle."

Suffice it to say, there's a strong argument for marketing and sales to work more closely together—and an even stronger one, when it comes to setting up your CRM and your salespeople for success.

When sales and marketing work together to ensure their CRM is integrated between their two departments, revenues and efficiencies can increase. *Imagine the possibilities.*

Wiley further expands on this idea, "Deep insight can be gained when sales and marketing data is aligned—quality benchmarks, conversion velocity, sales response efficiencies, the value of various marketing touches within the buyer's journey, etcetera."

Inter-department collaboration between sales, marketing, service, and support can become the lifeblood of an organization. Your CRM data can become the diagnostic tool to determine what is working and not working, and why.

Then departments work together to develop the key elements in the customization of their CRM setup, they increase the likelihood of their CRM providing customers, end users, and corporate leaders with what they need to help one another do better.

But the setup work is not done yet.

3. End-User Adaptation

Once the CRM technology is set up, the work is not complete. It would be like saying that once a child is born, the work is done. It's not. It is just the beginning, and as you know, it takes a village to raise a child. The same holds true for your CRM. It takes a village to set up a CRM.

As Todd Martin, VP Sales at Pipeliner CRM, says, "The CRM doesn't have to be done 100 percent to get started. Incrementally set it up so you can edit the system, edit the processes, see what works and what doesn't work, and gather more and more feedback from all departments."

A CRM is not static technology. It's agile technology that's meant to flex based on changes in your industry, your customer base and your team's and company's usage.

For this reason, check in with each level of your organization to ensure your CRM is still meeting their needs. For example, does the executive team find that the dashboard provides them with the information they need to make their decisions? Do you find that the system provides you with the reports and communication systems you need to help your team sell more? Do your salespeople find their individual reports helpful, and does their use of the CRM support or get in the way of the sale?

Wiley says, "Involve every level of the sales organization—from the inside sales reps to the SVP—when setting up a CRM."

Wiley shares how she met with individual salespeople to listen to calls to help determine if her team had accurately set up their CRM to identify qualified leads. She found that the way marketing defined a qualified lead was not the same as how the sales department defined a qualified lead. This demonstrates the value of marketing and sales working together.

By adapting your CRM to the end-users of your system, you can avoid these kinds of potential system glitches. *Let's hear it for the CRM village!*

The success of your CRM is in the details. Louis Fernandes, Director, Sales and Market Development at SAS, describes it for us, "It's how you use the technology, how you implement it, and how you adopt it that is most critical."

Successful CRM Usage

To ensure your CRM data is accurate and can be used effectively during your sales coaching, ensure that your team is using the technology appropriately. Rodrigo Vaca, VP Marketing at Zoho, says it well when he shares, "The success of a CRM is based on its usage."

Martin puts it, "The number one reason CRMs fail is because user adoption is not there."

There are three aspects your successful CRM usage:

1. Buy-In

As May's story illustrates, buy-in can be the key to your team's successful usage of your CRM. With this in mind, ensure you have fully socialized the importance of using your CRM. This takes more than a one-shot broadcasting of the benefits of using your CRM. Getting buy-in relies on an ongoing agile sale of the system.

Consider taking a coach-like approach in these discussions rather than a telling one. Ask what your team members understand as the reasons for the various parts of the CRM.

Get your team members talking about the benefits of your CRM and the *why* of using it. Help your team members discover what's in it for them. Martin adds, "Show salespeople that if they use the CRM, this is what they will get out of it."

Break things down from the big picture to how the information they enter affects and improves their world. Explore the function of the CRM and their role in the larger context so they understand how the information they enter impacts others in their organization.

Demonstrate what could happen if your team members enter inaccurate or no information. Discuss its effect on the organization and then bring it back to the impact on them.

2. Ease-of-Use

It's essential your CRM be easy for your salespeople to use. This ease-of-use is the necessary ingredient to your CRM's success. Vaca states, "Your CRM must be designed with the salesperson in mind. The goal is for salespeople to spend less time in the CRM and more time with customers."

Primarily, salespeople sell. I can hear you saying, "Yes, Peri, that's a no-brainer." Yet some organizations don't demonstrate they understand this with the structures they put into place. After selling, many salespeople perceive all other activities as secondary. To help your team members perform at their best, focus on simplifying the other aspects of their role.

Woollen explains, "Give your people tools. Make it [your CRM] mobile. Make it simple. Then, you can get them using it."

Make this your CRM customization mantra: "Simplify. Simplify. Simplify."

Vaca reminds us, "Your CRM must be designed to support the sales process." To illustrate his point, he shares his experience with their sales team when they made one simple change. They moved the location of the notes section of their CRM to the top of the screen.

The results? Their salespeople provided three times as many notes. This gave their company leaders more of the valuable customer information they wanted and needed.

In case you are wondering, Vaca's leaders provided no instructions. They simply just moved the location of their notes section. It begs the question, how can you customize your CRM (e.g., move the location of some material) so it's easier for your salespeople?

3. Client-Focused

It's a balancing act when customizing your CRM for your sales coaching. You want to ensure that your team members provide you with valuable information without negatively impacting their selling time, their customer relationships, or their results. At the same time, ensure that your team members provide enough of the right information in your CRM.

As Vaca says, "Set up your CRM to help sales reps get to know the customer better. For example, make the key information they need to get from the customer required information."

You want to have the best information at your fingertips so you can help your team members perform better, sales coach them more effectively, and give others in your company the information they need.

At the same time, you want to ensure that the way you have set up your system works for your buyers. With this in mind, occasionally take your CRM for a test drive from the client's perspective. This can be your cross check that you have set up your CRM in a client-focused fashion.

The success of your team members' CRM usage can be measured by their ownership for populating the CRM, and the quality of the data you and other leaders in your organization can mine from the system.

Successful Sales Coaching Setup

Just as corporate leaders can impact the success of a CRM's setup and usage, they can also affect the successful execution of sales coaching within their organization.

It comes down to what leaders are doing to create the corporate structure necessary to support a thriving sales coaching culture.

There are three basic areas to explore: time, priority, and systems.

1. Time

Every organization has a set of sales coaching time expectations, whether it's documented or not. It's just like every family has its holiday traditions. My parents had never overtly come out and said, "These are our family rituals," but my siblings and I accepted our traditions as reality. We learned what to expect from experience.

Your organization has an accepted sales coaching time length that is understood by your salespeople. It can range from 15 to 60 minutes. Its length is dependent on the complexity of the sales your team members are making, and the skill they possess.

There is a minimum frequency to your one-on-one sales coaching that will help your team members perform better. It's at least once a week. This seems to be the magic number when it comes to helping salespeople sell better. If you have new salespeople, you'll meet with them more frequently, but often for less time than you usually do with your other team members.

How you use that sales coaching time is also important and directly connects to your CRM. For example, what does your typical agenda look like? Where does the review of numbers fit in the agenda? And what proportion of your agenda is expected to be dedicated to reviewing the numbers?

2. Priority

The priority an organization gives to sales coaching is often indicated in the small details. Some organizations go so far as to have dedicated sales coaching rooms in every sales department.

One of the telltale signs that an organization is committed to sales coaching is that one-on-one sales coaching is scheduled into every salesperson's and sales manager's agenda.

Another indicator of a company's sales coaching health is measured by how far in advance sales coaching is booked. I've worked with a very successful sales manager who had his sales coaching sessions booked 12 months in advance with each of his team members. This might seem a bit excessive, but at least his team knew he was dedicated to their success.

When it comes to demonstrating that sales coaching is a priority, it's often helpful for sales managers to have a policy of not cancelling sales coaching sessions, but rather of rescheduling them. This lets your team members know their sales coaching time with you is a priority.

3. Systems

Based on the nature of organizations, what gets systemized is often what gets done. With this in mind, leaders can support their sales managers in their coaching role by creating systems and structure to facilitate sales coaching sessions.

This can simply be done by clarifying and documenting what percentage of a sales manager's time is expected to be spent on coaching. I've often been surprised by the variance in response rates when sales VPs and managers are asked what percentage of their time is expected to be spent sales coaching. There was considerable variation in percentages expected by the sales VPs and sales managers. Responses have ranged from 80 percent to 20 percent in the same company.

Leaders can help support a system-wide commitment to sales coaching by clearly delineating what percentage of time managers should spend on it. Clearly stating the time expectations in job descriptions and any respective workforce management technology creates standards, so at least there is a minimum sales coaching time that sales managers can work to achieve.

If you are a leader trying to decide how to best help your sales managers coach more effectively, look closely at the structure your company uses to determine its sales coaching time, priority, and systems. How can you demonstrate to your sales division that you respect sales coaching?

Since coaching has been identified as a significant driver to increase sales, it makes sense for organizations to ensure they create the structure to support a robust sales coaching culture.

Bad News

I have some bad news for you: You could set up your CRM well, and your team could be using it as they should. And, you could be working in a company that provides the structure to support your sales coaching. These three will definitely help make leveraging your CRM during sales coaching much easier, but they don't guarantee your success. You want to avoid one mistake many sales managers make.

Before we go there, let's digress for a moment. It'll illustrate how to better leverage your CRM during sales coaching.

Your CRM can be your Mr. Spock. Wait, did I just bring in *Star Trek? Yes, I did.* (And no, I'm not a Trekkie.)

Your CRM can be like your Mr. Spock during your sales coaching. Remember how Mr. Spock became an indispensable, trustworthy partner to Captain Kirk. Mr. Spock was consulted when major decisions were being made. He was often an unbiased observer, an information gatherer—and could provide the data when someone needed it.

Your CRM can be the same for you. It can be your sidekick to help you make better decisions. It can be an unbiased witness to what is working and not working for your team members. It can provide information that you wouldn't be able to gather otherwise, when and where your team needs it.

Keep the picture of your CRM as Mr. Spock in your mind. Now, let's go back to the mistake many sales managers commit when it comes to using their CRMs during sales coaching.

Let's Agree

The biggest mistake sales managers make when using their CRM during sales coaching is: *They coach the numbers, not the people.*

What does this look like?

These sales managers enter coaching sessions with their carefully charted CRM numbers in hand, and talk about the data as if talking can change them. They talk about last week's or last month's numbers. They talk about the pipeline. They talk about the sales forecast. They talk about which sales numbers are trending up, and which ones are going down. And, they incent the results they want to improve.

Does any of this sound familiar? If it does, you're not alone. Many organizations "coach the numbers," and many sales managers have been taught to do so. It's so common that many salespeople have experienced it, and some might expect it in coaching.

This is about to change for you. Shortly, you're going to learn the six ways to leverage your CRM during your sales coaching.

Let's go back to your CRM as Mr. Spock. If you only coach the numbers, it would be like *only* having Mr. Spock available to your team members. No disrespect to Mr. Spock, but his powerful position existed because of his contrast to Captain Kirk. Mr. Spock was the logic, and Captain Kirk was the human connection.

Your CRM works in a similar way. Without you and the human dynamic you bring to the table through your trusting relationship with your team members, your sales conversations get reduced to a logical "coaching of the numbers." And, you decrease the likelihood of having much influence over your team's performance.

Think of it this way: How much impact would Mr. Spock *alone* have had on the universe? I'd suggest not much. It was the power of the dynamic duo of Mr. Spock *and* Captain Kirk that changed the universe.

The same holds true for your CRM and you in sales coaching. Together you make a dynamic duo that can change your team's sales world.

Now, let's go back to why you don't want to coach the numbers.

Here's the Problem

The problem with only coaching the numbers is that it doesn't produce the ongoing, incremental sales improvement that can occur when more effective sales coaching is executed.

If you only coach the numbers, you're not helping your team members identify or improve their sales behaviors that led to those numbers.

If you don't identify those behaviors, you won't know how to help your team members do improve their sales behaviors to get better results.

If you don't identify the sales behaviors behind their numbers, you won't be able to discover the thinking behind their actions.

And if you don't discover the thinking behind their sales behaviors, you'll be less likely to influence the thinking that drove the behaviors that caused the results.

Are you with me? If not, you may want to reread that.

When you only coach the numbers, you're limited to a coaching strategy that is based on hope rather than the true driver of sales success. Hope is not a sales coaching strategy that produces results. Coaching the numbers reduces your sales coaching to a conversation of hope for sales improvement.

The Forensic Evidence

The following forensic evidence includes some of the clues left behind when sales managers only coach the numbers.

Use the forensic evidence as a guideline to help you identify if you're coaching the numbers and losing sight of the people. As you know, identifying if you coach the numbers is not about labeling, but rather helping you improve the use of your CRM during sales coaching.

Sales Numbers and Statistics – The potential statistical evidence.

Sales plateau.
Sales trend downwards.
Sales numbers are not predictable.

Observable Prospect/Client Behavior – The potential prospect/client evidence.

Complains about lack of customization.
Talks about poor service.
Does not demonstrate loyalty to company or product.
May complain about price.

(continued)

(continued)

Observable Team Member Behavior – The potential evidence your team members exhibit in general.

> *Tries to engage clients using only numbers to make their buying decisions.*
> *Does not connect with clients' emotional reasons for buying.*
> *Stresses about meeting numbers.*
> *Focuses on number of sales made, not relationships with clients.*

Observable Coaching Behavior – The potential evidence your team members exhibit in coaching sessions.

> *Tends to provide answers with little or no depth of understanding of clients' needs.*
> *Has trouble answering questions about how they engaged clients.*
> *Ask for help with how to deal with price objections.*

Your Observable Behavior – The potential evidence you exhibit.

> *Leave coaching until the numbers come in.*
> *Determine who to coach based on numbers.*
> *Use most of your coaching time to review the numbers with team members.*
> *Discuss client experience as secondary to sales numbers.*

What to Watch and Listen for in Your Sales Coaching

Cloud, social, and mobile technologies have changed the way people buy, which alters the way your salespeople sell, which shifts the way you sales coach. As Nick Stein, Senior Director, Marketing and Communications at Salesforce Work.com, so aptly puts it, "These technologies have made the world move much faster, and companies who don't adapt will get left behind."

Gschwandtner describes this new sales reality, "Sales 2.0 is the marriage between people, processes, and technology. And what we need to be effective is to align all three."

John Seeds, Marketing Director at Parature, states, "Because of the proliferation of the resources at a customer's disposal, you now have to differentiate yourself in a way that your product moves from being a commodity to a solution."

Salesperson's Role

This technological shift dictates a change in the role of the salesperson. Instead of providing information in a shotgun effect, salespeople are required to provide relevant information in an elegant, concise way to prospects with varying needs, wherever they are in their buying decisions. This can be like a matching game. (For more on how to actually coach your team members to do this, review Chapters 3 and 8.)

Gschwandtner adds, "Today sales is about helping customers come to insights they wouldn't have come to on their own."

Fernandes describes, "The salesperson's role now is more of a facilitator or orchestrator."

Greenberg expands on the idea. "Stop pitching stuff at prospects and instead start asking them about the outcomes they are looking for." He further states, "The fundamental focus on relationship remains a constant." (Remember Chapter 10?)

To add to these changes, social technology can provide salespeople with valuable information to better understand customers' needs and deliver on these outcomes. Seeds expands on the value of social information for salespeople, "Social profile has become more and more important to integrate so you understand a particular sales lead."

Greenberg shares his perception of this new sales world, "The thing to consider is how sales has changed based on what customers demand and require now for not only closing but for post-sale interaction. This changes the nature of the salesperson as well as their methodology of approaches, techniques, and tool usage."

Sales Manager's Role

These changes in the salesperson's world dictate a change in the sales manager's role. Stein shares, "The way many companies are managing their people and performance processes are often still stuck in old world hierarchy."

Help your team sell more in this new sales reality with these three basic steps:

1. Ensure you're not coaching the numbers.
2. Coach your team to become stellar salespeople. (Use the forensic evidence, ideas, and sales coaching questions in this book to assist you.)
3. Help your team members sell more effectively with the use of social media.

Ensure your salespeople focus on helping others with their buying decisions, wherever they are in their decision-making process. Coach your team members to the point that they can flawlessly match your company's information to the needs of their prospects.

When you coach your team members on their use of social media, help them better understand their customers. As Martin says, "Use social to really educate salespeople on who their buyers are."

Use the power of your CRM's integration to improve your sales coaching and help your team members sell more. It increases the quality, speed, and value of the information you and they glean from the system. It might just give you back some much needed time and your team members more ways to collaborate with others in the company to sell more. Vaca shares this value with his clear statement, "Integrate your CRM."

Woollen shares how an integrated CRM can facilitate the completion of more sales in a more efficient manner. "The best salespeople . . . are very good at influencing the other parts of their organization. . . . This is where collaboration becomes key and the sharing of information important."

Utilize your system to facilitate collaboration and sharing within your company. This is what Woollen was referring to earlier when he spoke of a CRM moving from a reporting system to a selling system.

If your organization is truly dedicated to creating a sales coaching culture, coach your salespeople to sell more, and helping customers with their buying decisions can anchor your CRM to your organization's DNA. Stein summaries, "The goal is to make sales coaching scalable and part of everyday workflow."

If you aren't already doing it, add remote sales coaching to your repertoire. The sales coaching ideas shared in this book work just as well when employed virtually. A larger portion of my meetings are happening virtually, and if you're not yet comfortable with mobile and virtual technologies that allow you to coach your team members from anywhere, do yourself a favor and gain a level of greater ease.

If you are comfortable with using technology for remote sales coaching, challenge yourself and work on developing your virtual trust-building strategy (see Chapter 1 to learn more about the value of trust to sales coaching).

Leverage Your CRM during Sales Coaching

Since sales coaching is about helping your salespeople sell more and your CRM measures the level of your team members' sales success, you'll find it helpful to better integrate your CRM into your sales coaching. What May says about measurement is true—what gets measured gets done. But beware when you use your CRM during sales coaching, not to fall for coaching the numbers.

Instead, use the numbers as the springboard for your sales coaching conversation. Use the numbers to discover the behaviors that are responsible for the numbers. As your team members talk about the behaviors they have and haven't engaged in, find out what they did well and what sales mistakes they have made. This will provide you with rich material for productive and profitable sales coaching conversations.

Here are six ways to leverage your CRM during sales coaching:

1. Your CRM as a Springboard

The individual sales reports you get can serve as an excellent springboard into a sales coaching conversation when the numbers indicate there has been a change in performance from one recording period to the next.

Under these circumstances you can use what I call the Compare-and-Contrast Model for Improved Thinking. It's actually quite simple. As the title implies, your team members would compare and contrast what they did differently to get the different results.

Let's say your team member, Suzanna, has just come off a month where her sales were down 20 percent from the previous month. You would ask her questions to compare and contrast what she did or didn't do differently last versus the previous month. Team members are usually able to isolate what is that they did that got them the better results.

Your side of the compare-and-contrast conversation might sound like this:

"Let's contrast at your sales results from the previous month to this past month." (*You place the results in front of her so she can see the two at the same time.*)

"What do you notice?"

"What did you do the previous month that got you those results?"

"What did or didn't you do differently last month?" (*Usually a lightbulb will go off after you ask this question, and your team member will realize what they stopped doing or what they did that got in the way of their sales.*)

"What do you think you can do to bring your numbers back up this coming month?" (*Notice the emphasis on what Suzanna is going to do to change the numbers not just that she is going to change the numbers. That would be considered coaching the numbers.*)

As you know from the previous chapters in this book, you can then use the behaviors behind your team members' numbers to coach their thinking. And ultimately, improve their results.

2. Your CRM as a Prioritization Tool

You can use your CRM to help your team members prioritize their sales actions. In our programs, we often talk about the value of clarifying with team members what their top priorities are.

Experience has demonstrated that salespeople often are not working on what their manager thinks are their priorities. In these circumstances, there's sometimes a disconnect between what salespeople think are priorities and what experienced sales managers know are more productive priorities.

For example, you can do this by reviewing your team members' leads and prioritizing their action steps accordingly.

You can do this simply by asking:

"Which leads are you planning on focusing on today/tomorrow/this week?"

"What made you decide to choose those?"

"What made you decide not to follow up on those?"

"In general, how do you decide on your priorities for the day?"

By using your CRM as a prioritization tool, you help your salespeople be more efficient with their management of their time so they can maximize their performance and results.

3. Your CRM as a Feedback Tool

You can use your CRM during sales coaching to objectively measure the impact of your team members' new sales behaviors. Think back to guideline number 5 from Chapter 12. You end each of your coaching conversations with your team member's commitment to one new sales approach that will have the greatest impact on their sales.

Your CRM can be the feedback tool to measure how successful that new approach really is. It provides you and your team members with the metrics to say definitively, "Yes, that new approach really works."

Research indicates that when providing feedback, it's more effective for most people if feedback is provided in the context of the individual's previous performance not compared to the performance of the whole team. With this in mind, determine the context in which you're going to provide each of your team members with feedback.

When using your CRM as a feedback tool, your side of the conversation can include:

"Let's take a peek at your numbers over the last two weeks and see if your new approach has had any impact." (*You both look over the numbers for that individual for the last two weeks.*)

"Where would you expect to see a difference in your numbers because of this new sales approach you've been using?"

"What do you notice?"

"What kind of difference did it make from your previous numbers?:

Using your CRM as a feedback tool during your sales coaching can help your team members really understand and get the connection between their new sales approaches and their improved numbers.

Depending on how your team members are compensated, you may also want to ask questions to help them realize how continuing with their new sales behavior affects their compensation.

4. Your CRM as a Crystal Ball

Salespeople and sales managers often discuss pipeline and forecasting. When you use your CRM as your crystal ball, you can measure how realistic and accurate you and your team members are in these activities.

You'll quickly discover how large the gap is between your team members' planned numbers and their actual numbers. You'll begin to know who is the most realistic when they set their personal targets. Ideally, you want the gap between their plans and their actual numbers to be as close as possible. It's like your ideal weight versus your actual weight. Your goal is to have them as close as possible to one another.

To help your team members become more aware of the gap between their plans and their actual numbers, you might ask questions like:

"Let's look the personal sales goals you set the last few times we met. How close are your planned versus your actual numbers?"

"Do you notice any patterns?" (*Let's say your team member says yes.*)

"What patterns do you notice?"

"What insight can you gain from that?"

"How will that affect the goal you set for this coming week?"

When you use your CRM as a crystal ball, you help your salespeople set more accurate personal sales goals, and narrow the gap between their projected and actual numbers.

5. Your CRM as a Report Card

Your CRM can function as a report card for each of your team members. *And no, they don't have to take it home to get signed.* They can use it as a snapshot of how they are doing so the two of you can engage in a sales coaching conversation and set out a plan for greater improvement.

To build your relationships with your team members, when you use your CRM as a report card, keep the discussion focused on your team members' higher numbers. Then, transition the conversation to identifying their best practices and exploring if they have an interest in mentoring or peer coaching.

You have the library within your CRM to help your team members share best practices with one another and other department members.

Be on the lookout for not only best practices but also best stories that can be documented to help others on the team better respond to objections, engage prospects more fully, and make the ideas they share more memorable.

Your CRM as a report card questions might include:

"Let's look at your numbers over the past month or two. Which numbers do you notice are consistently above target?"

"What have you been doing to get such high numbers?"

"Can you tell more about how you do that?"

"And then what do you do next?"

"That's the first time I've heard of anyone doing that. What a great idea! How would you feel about sharing that at our next sales meeting?"

When team members discuss what they are doing to get the great results they're getting, it can build the relationship between you. As you may recall, trust is an essential ingredient to your team members performing better, you knowing more accurately what is happening on your team, and clients being treated better by your team members. (For a refresher on this, reread Chapter 1.)

6. Your CRM as a Stethoscope

As you know, listening to customers is key to sales success. When you use your CRM as a stethoscope during sales coaching, you and your team members can discover more about customers by gathering valuable social information about their leads.

For example, when was the last time that you coached one of your salespeople on how they use LinkedIn as a prospecting tool?

Your CRM as a stethoscope questions might include:

"What social source are you using to connect with prospects?"

"Which of those gives you the best results?" (*If your team members aren't sure, together discover the answer with your social CRM.*)

"Can you walk me through the steps of how you have been using LinkedIn?"

"What information are you looking for when you research a lead?"

"How do you use their previous positions to help you better understand how to approach them?"

"How to you make the initial contact?"

"What do you do once they accept your invite to connect?"

The social aspect of selling is a great way to listen and learn about prospects. By using your CRM as a stethoscope, you help your team members better understand what is valuable and relevant sales information in prospects' social profiles.

CRM Preparation for Sales Mistake Prevention

As you know, when you prevent your team members from committing sales mistakes, they'll sell more. For the final exercise, integrate the ideas from this book with your company's CRM metrics to create a sales mistake prevention chart. (Remember, you can get a printable version of this and the 10 other sales exercises from this book at www.CoachingandSalesInstitute.com.)

Follow these simple instructions and the sales mistake prevention chart will become a valuable tool to helping your team sell more:

1. Review the forensic evidence section from Chapters 2 through 11. You'll discover the general metrics to determine which mistakes are being committed by your team.

2. With the forensic evidence from each of the mentioned chapters as your guide, fill out Column 2 of the following sales mistake prevention chart using the metrics that you and your company use.

3. Using the sample sales coaching questions from Chapters 2 through 11, write in the questions you would ask your team members about the details of each sales mistake in Column 3.

4. Using the content from Chapters 2 through 11, make a brief note about the key ideas that are most relevant to help your team members overcome the corresponding sales mistake in Column 4.

Sales Mistake Prevention Chart

Column 1	Column 2	Column 3	Column 4
Chapter and Sales Mistake	Which of your company metrics indicate the sales mistake (listed in Column 1) is occurring?	What questions can you ask to discover the details of what your team member did?	What ideas will prevent your team members from committing this sales mistake?
Chapter 2: Not Being Clear Who's Buying			
Chapter 3: Forgetting Why People Buy			
Chapter 4: Being Self-Focused			
Chapter 5: Telling Mistruths			
Chapter 6: Being Ill-Prepared			
Chapter 7: Taking Too Much of the Client's Time			
Chapter 8: Sharing What's Not Relevant			
Chapter 9: Missing Prospects' Buying Cues			
Chapter 10: Acting like a Traditional Salesperson			
Chapter 11: Treating Clients as Enemies			

Review the stats for each team member with the assistance of your sales mistake prevention chart (once you have filled it out). You'll quickly discover which mistakes your salespeople are most likely committing. Leverage the chart during your sales coaching, in partnership with the ideas from the corresponding chapter, to help your team members do better and sell more.

Action Items from This Chapter

1. Set up your CRM for success.
2. Ensure your team is using your CRM well.
3. Be a champion of creating the structure for a thriving and profitable sales coaching culture.
4. Don't coach the numbers.
5. Prepare for the dynamic power of Mr. Spock and Captain Kirk (your CRM and you).
6. Use the six ways to leverage your CRM during sales coaching.
7. Fill out the Sales Mistake Prevention Chart
8. Keep the Sales Mistake Prevention Chart handy when you're using your CRM and when you're sales coaching.
9. Review the Sales Mistake Prevention Chart regularly to diagnose the sales mistakes being committed by your salespeople.
10. Use the information from this book to better leverage your CRM during sales coaching.

ABOUT THE AUTHOR

Peri Shawn is a sales coaching thought leader who transforms the complexity of getting your salespeople to perform better into the fewest number of action steps to sell more. Peri's company, the Coaching and Sales Institute (CSI), has been in the sales coaching business for 25 years, and is behind the launch of such products as the debit card and BlackBerry in Canada.

Peri has also authored three corporate guidebooks: *The Sales Coaching Guide: 150 Coaching Tips for Sales Leaders to Increase Sales*; *The Sales Guide: 150 Tips for Salespeople to Sell More, Better, Sooner and More Often*; and, *The Coaching Guide: 150 Tips for Managers to Increase Performance and Productivity*. She is the brains behind CSI's two virtual programs: *Mark's Academy*, an engaging, animated sales training series designed to help salespeople in the new business reality; and *Coaching for Better Results*, a program for leaders to develop their coaching skills and fully integrate *The Secret Formula for Coaching Questions* into their daily practice.

Peri provides coaching, sales coaching, and sales programs for sales executives, sales managers, and salespeople. In this role, she has been in the unique position of observing and coaching scores of sales coaching sessions and meetings.

As part of Peri's ongoing research, she has developed groundbreaking proprietary tools that demonstrate how trust affects performance, management, and the client experience. She is the author of over 20 sales and coaching tools created to help leaders coach their teams to sell better. These include the CSI Trust Survey, the Sales Coaching Audit, and the Coaching Indicators.

To sign up for Peri's Sales Coaching Tips, get her help with your team's performance, or to book her for your next in-person or virtual event, reach her at www.CoachingandSalesInstitute.com.

INDEX

Alternative close technique, 133
Asking meaningful questions, 11
Awareness of declining interest, 98

Best interests of people, holding in mind,
    71–72
Biases, sales and sales coaching, 1, 65
Bottom-line versions of sales conversa-
    tions, 99
Brainstorming:
    noticing buying cues, 124–125
    respecting time factors, 102–103
Buying criteria, identifying, 27–28
Buying cues:
    brainstorming, 124–125
    engaging prospects in conversations,
       125–126
    importance of recognizing, 122–123
    missing, 119–122
    motivating for next time, 126
    noticing, 124
    preparation for recognizing, 128–129
    sales coaching questions for, 126–128
    watching and listening for, 123–124

Celine Effect, 160, 168
Choice, providing to clients, 100–101
Client-focus:
    being self-focused, 47–50
    in communications, 57–58
    of CRM, 175
    customizing needs, 56–57

demonstrating, 57
importance of, 50–52
preparation for, 60
questions for, 52–56
sales coaching questions for, 58–59
traditional sales approach compared to,
    137–138
watching and listening for, 52
Close, going for, compared to helping with
    buying decisions, 137–138
Coaching:
    allocation of time spent in, 8–9
    baking cake compared to, 2
    benefits of, 3–5
    CRM setup for, 175–177
    explaining why of, 164–165
    leveraging CRM during, 177–180,
       182–189
    making sustainable, 159–168
    mistakes in, 166
    people, not numbers, 177–180
    as right and privilege, 1
    watching and listening for, 20, 37, 52,
       68, 83, 97, 111, 123, 135, 149, 180
Commitments, including in coaching, 163
Communication:
    client-focus in, 57–58
    follow-up, customizing, 153–154
    of product knowledge, 73
    stiff and scripted compared to well-
      prepared, 83–84
Consistency and trust, 71

Conversations:
  engaging prospects in, 125–126
  focusing on in coaching, 162
  having profitable, 138–139
CRM:
  buy-in, 173–174
  client-focused, 175
  company strategy with, 171
  ease-of-use, 174
  end-user adaptation, 172–173
  implementation, 169–170
  inter-department collaboration with,
    171–172
  leveraging during coaching, 177–180,
    182–187
  preparation for sales mistake preven-
    tion, 187–189
  priority given to coaching, 176
  sales coaching setup, 175–177
  setup, 170–173
  systems, 176–177
  time expectations of coaching, 175–176
  usage, 169–170, 173–175
Culture, trust-based, 70–72, 139
Customizing client needs, 56–57

Decision makers:
  clarifying role of, 23–24
  focusing on decision-making processes,
    20–23
  identifying buying criteria, 27–28
  isolating steps in decision-making pro-
    cess, 25–27
  misidentifying, 17–20
  preparation for clarifying, 29–30
  role of others in decision-making,
    24–25
  sales coaching questions for, 28–29
Definition of sales, clarifying, 74–75

E-mails, 57–58
Emotional reasons for buying, 39–40
Enemies, treating clients as. See Treatment
  of prospects
Engaging clients in storytelling, 43

Exercises for sales coaches, 13–14
Expectations related to time, managing,
  101–102
Explaining why of coaching, 164–165

Feedback:
  building into coaching, 166–167
  CRM as tool for, 184–185
  demonstrating understanding of,
    98–99
Follow-up
  to coaching, 163–164
  to communication, 153–154
Forgetting why people buy. See Reasons for
  buying

Gladwell, Malcolm, *Outliers*, 81

Helping:
  clients with buying decisions, 137–138
  team members, 162–163
Hidden processes or procedures, objections
  to, 87

Ill-prepared, being. See Preparation
Industry buying cues, 124–125
Information. See also Sharing relevant
  information
  supplying, 11–12
  targeted, 88–89
Interest, declining, 98
Interrogation, avoiding, 162

Judgment zone, staying out of, 124, 126

Leveraging:
  CRM during coaching, 177–180,
    182–187
  technology to determine information
    need, 89
Listening:
  assessing current level of, 9–10
  to discover sales mistakes, 153
  importance of, 8–9
  in-the-moment feedback on, 10

to share relevant information, 112
trust and, 10–11, 71
Logical reasons for buying, 40–41

Manipulative sales techniques. *See*
Traditional approach to sales
Mirror neurons, 70–71, 137–138
Mistakes:
being ill-prepared, 79–92
being self-focused, 47–60
forgetting why people buy, 33–46
missing buying cues, 119–129
not being clear who's buying, 17–30
not sharing relevant information,
107–117
taking too much time, 93
taking traditional sales approach,
131–142
telling mistruths, 63–78
treating clients as enemies, 145–156
Mistruths. *See* Truthfulness
Motivating team members for next time,
126

Objections, helping clients with, 28,
87–88
Opinions, giving, 83, 85–86
OSF (Oh-So-Familiar) Cycle, 6–7
Others, role of in decision-making process,
24–25

Pains, exploring, 54–55
Passions, exploring, 54
PERI sales story formula, 42–43
Pitch personality, 138–139
Power dynamics, engaging in, 87
Preparation:
answering questions, 86
being ill-prepared, 79–81
coaching for, 84–85
giving opinions, 85–86
importance of, 81–82
knowing what information clients want,
88–89
planning and, 91–92

responding to objections, 87–88
sales coaching questions for, 90
stiff and scripted compared to well-
prepared, 83–84
watching and listening for, 83
Priorities, exploring, 54
Product knowledge:
discovering, 72–74
preparation for, 77–78
Prospect buying cues. *See* Buying cues
Ps of questions, 54–55

Quantum Coaching Effect, 5, 167–168
Questions:
answering, 86
guidelines for, 161–165
Questions, asking meaningful
to demonstrate competence, 55–56
to discover client needs, 52–55
open-ended questions, 101
pain questions, 54–55
for sales coaching, 11, 160–161

Reasons for buying:
forgetting, 33–35
identifying, 38–41
importance of, 35–36
linking to products, 41
listening for, 38
preparation for remembering, 45–46
sales coaching questions for, 44–45
transactions compared to sales, 36–37
watching and listening for, 37–38
Relationships with clients, building, 83
Relevancy. *See* Sharing relevant
information
Results from products, as reasons for
buying, 42–43

Sales, clarifying definition of, 74–75
Sales manager, role of, 181–182
Salesperson, role of, 181
Self-focus. *See* Client-focus
Sensitivity to time concerns. *See* Time
factors in conversations

Sharing relevant information:
  illustration of, 114
  importance of, 110–111
  listening, 112
  not sharing, 107–109
  preparation for, 115–117
  providing belief or understanding, 113
  sales coaching questions for, 114–115
  watching and listening for, 111–112
Short versions of sales conversations, 99
Social media, 66, 89
Storytelling, 42–43
Stress and brain function, 69–70
Struggle, benefits of, 5–8, 160
Success, as contagious, 167–168

Technology, leveraging to determine information need, 89
Theory, avoiding discussions of, 161–162
Thinking behind behaviors, focusing on, 1
Time factors in conversations:
  accomplishing, 99–100
  being specific with clients, 101
  hearing feedback, 98–99
  importance of, 96–97
  managing client expectations, 101–102
  meeting idea and, 102–103
  preparation for, 104–105
  providing clients with choice, 100–101
  sales coaching questions for, 103–104
  taking too much time, 93–95
  watching and listening for, 97–98
Traditional approach to sales:
  developing trust compared to, 139–140
  having profitable conversations compared to, 138–139

helping clients with buying decisions compared to, 137–138
  preparation of alternatives to, 141–142
  preventing, 136–137
  problem with, 134–135
  sales coaching questions for, 140–141
  taking, 131–134
  watching and listening for, 135–136
Treatment of prospects:
  customizing follow-up communication, 153–154
  as enemies, 145–149
  example of, 150–151
  as friends, 152–153
  preparation for friendly treatment, 156
  sales coaching questions for, 154–156
  watching and listening for, 149–150
Trust. *See also* Truthfulness
  importance of, 10–11
  traditional sales techniques and, 133–134, 139–140
Truthfulness:
  admitting to lack of, 75
  creating trust-based sales culture, 70–72
  defining sales, 74–75
  discovering product knowledge, 72–74
  importance of, 66–68
  preparation for product knowledge, 77–78
  sales coaching questions for, 75–77
  as situational, 69–70
  telling mistruths, 63–66
  trust and, 68–69

Voice messages, 57–58